Common Sense in Poker

Common Sense in Poker

by **Irwin Steig**

Illustrated by William Steig

CORNERSTONE LIBRARY   NEW YORK

Reprinted 1978

This new Cornerstone Library edition is a complete
and unabridged reprint of the original hardcover edition.

Manufactured in the United States of America
under the supervision of
Rolls Offset Printing Co., Inc., N.Y.

To my friend, Willy Van Roosbroeck—

mathematical scientist, chess player, poker player, wit.

Contents

Common Sense in Poker

1

About You

Since I am proposing, by means of questions and answers, to point the way to increased Poker profit for you, I think it will help to start with two questions about you, so that I can prove I know you.

If, on being presented to you in person, I promptly proceeded to quiz you about yourself, the chances are you would tell me, politely or facetiously or indignantly, to mind my own business. And you would be justified in resenting the breach of your privacy.

But here you can answer to yourself. No revenue agent will hear you and start asking follow-up questions; no friend will hear you and start needling. My job here is to help you win money at Poker, so I hope you will be frank, because you have nobody to kid but yourself.

1. At Poker, do you: Win most of the time? Just about break even? Lose most of the time?

2. Why?

If I could hear your answer to the first question, I would be willing to bet — to give you 9 to 1 odds — on my ability to predict your answer to the second. Am I clairvoyant? No, statistical. Over the years, I have heard from hundreds of Poker players — all types in all classes — explanations of their performance. I have kept records. Accordingly, I think I know what explanation to expect from you after you have told how you fare.

Let us see if I am right about you.

If you answered, truthfully, that you win most of the time, you probably attribute the phenomenon to your skill; otherwise you are too modest. After hauling in pot after pot over the course of a session, you may say, "I was lucky," but you won't mean it. You may say it because you feel embarrassed taking all that loot from your friends, although you have earned it by outplaying them. Or the rascal in you may be emerging: you may want to shore up their hopes so that they will return next week to give you more chips. Being a consistent winner, you hardly need my help, but I hope you will find it entertaining to continue and to check your ideas against mine.

If you answered that you just about break even, please reconsider — ransack your memory for some of the clobberings you have absorbed. Most card players are optimists; the man who says he breaks even over the long pull is, as a rule, practicing self-delusion. In any case, you probably said next, "It is a matter of luck."

If you admitted that you lose most of the time, it is virtually certain that you are convinced your luck is bad, and the cards are to blame. My thesis is that, if you usually pay out at Poker, the reason is that you continually *invite* what you call your bad luck, and by your actions compel it to stay with you —

You repeatedly throw away your money —

You are like the man who rows out to the middle of a lake, flings coins overboard, and considers himself unlucky when they sink —

But you can make your luck good without sleight of hand, or rabbits' feet, or other devices for courting the occult —

You can make the cards love you —

You can win most of the time by applying always certain simple strategic and tactical principles, about which most players, including the veterans, know next to nothing.

In short, my thesis is that you can win as easily as you lose.

To prove my point, I am inviting you to a seven-hand game—to sit in with six other players, each of them typical of millions the nation over.

One is an expert.

Two are better than average.

Two are below average (and the national average is pitiable).

One is completely inept.

Later, still another below-average player will sit in.

So, if with valid reason you hold your brand of Poker in high esteem, you will be getting all the better of it here, at the same time encountering enough competent opposition to test you. But if you have not been doing so well as you would like, you will not be too far beyond your depth; you should, in fact, be able to outmaneuver some of the opposition.

The stakes will be up to the limit of what you can afford:

just high enough to make a juicy win worthwhile and a severe beating sting. They will be stated in terms of chips. Please think about each chip in terms of money significant to you.

You will be asked to play dealer's choice: the most popular variations of Draw and Stud, natural and with wild cards (within reason), one-winner and high-low.

In each variation, you will be confronted with series of basic problems exploring every phase of that variation. The answers in the text will be accompanied by the reasoning. Where necessary, the applicable odds will be given.

All the essential tables of odds will be included in Chapter 18 entitled "The Structure of Poker." Review them, if you will, before you tackle the problems, or leave them for later, or use them for reference, or ignore them. Far be it for me to suggest that you bone up on them and use them to win bets.

The cards are being shuffled. Of course, you want some information about the opposition, so I shall tell you who is what in this group. As I introduce each player, I shall whisper something about him in your ear.*

*If you've never played Poker before, now is a good time to read Chapter 17, "The Essential Rules."

2

From the Gallery

Seated clockwise around the table are Potzer, Guffy, Wad, Mouse, Showbuck, Brill. As you vie with them, you will soon realize they are not strangers— that they are incarnations of players you have often met. You will readily identify them as prototypes from the vast Poker gallery. You will observe in each one traits of some regular in your own group back home.

Potzer is a cheerful little man, a veteran bungler. He plays in every pot — stays as long as there is the slimmest chance of his winning it, and often stays when it should be obvious he has no chance at all. He does not make the same error twice; he makes it hundreds of times. Don't try to read logic into anything he does.

Guffy is a chatterbox, often witty, sometimes banal. His

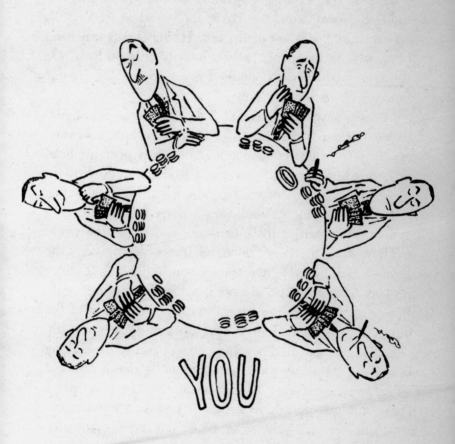

YOU

best sallies are usually directed at himself. His Poker technique is excellent. His chattering is his weakness, for it abounds in tells. The most damaging of these is that he becomes silent when he holds a cinch hand.

Wad is the wealthiest member of the group, and the tightest — away from the Poker table and at it. Wasting no chips, he keeps out of the red. He stays only when his prospects are excellent; he bets heavily only on locks. On the average, he throws one bluff every six months. He can be bluffed when he is losing.

Mouse knows plenty about Poker but little about prudence. Although the stakes set by this group are beyond his means, he insists on playing. Being in over his head has made him cautious — too cautious. He sees nonexistent traps, and folds too often. He jabs when he should slug. A modest raise by him indicates a powerful hand.

Showbuck owns a thick bankroll, and wants the world to know it. At the Poker table, his status-seeking takes the form of rash bets. He may annoy you by making it costly for you to finish second in a pot in which he finishes fourth. If you say he spoils the game, you are losing sight of the object: to win chips. He is, in effect, begging you to win his.

Brill is genial at all times, and you will find yourself liking him. He is genuinely warm and outgoing — that is his most valuable personal asset. Do not be deceived by it: he plays Poker ruthlessly. He is an authentic expert: a rapid calculator and shrewd psychologist. When you stay in a pot with him, be sure your hand warrants your doing so, because Brill will not be in it unless he is off to an excellent start.

Now I am going to ask you to sit down with Potzer immediately to your left and Brill immediately to your right. Unless you are different from most Poker players, you should like that. Most players would rather draw before the persistent stayer than after him. They remember how often he has drawn off, to no purpose, the card they had hoped to catch; they forget how often he has drawn off a card they could not use, thereby giving them another chance.

Guffy has just piped up: "Are we going to gab forever? Deal, somebody!"

Coming from Guffy, that is a boffola.

To Open or Not to Open
QUESTIONS

Among the last several generations of Poker players, Jackpots has been the most popular form of Draw. To open, you need one pair of J's, or better. On the average, such a holding — something from one pair of J's all the way up through a royal flush* — occurs once in approximately five hands. Equipped with this information, or having casually dismissed it from your mind, you hear the dealer make his choice: "Jacks or better." Everybody antes one chip. You may open for two chips, and raises are limited to two chips. What do you do in each of the following situations?

1. Brill deals. You are under the gun, that is, the first player required to act. You hold J J A 9 6. Open or check?

2. Again, you are under the gun. You hold Q Q J 9 8. Open or check?

3. And again, you are under the gun. You hold J J 10 9 8. Open or check?

4. Showbuck deals. Brill checks. You hold 10 10 9 9 8. Open or check?

*See "Glossary" at end of book, if necessary, for explanation of this and other Poker terminology.

5. Wad deals. Mouse, Showbuck, and Brill check. You hold K K A 4 2. Open or check?

6. Mouse deals. Showbuck and Brill check. You hold J J 3 3 2. Open or check?

7. Brill deals. Once again, you are under the gun. You hold 4 4 4 4 J, and nothing has been said about royalties, so you must assume there won't be any. Open or check?

8. Wad deals. Mouse, Showbuck, and Brill check. You hold J J 6 4 2. Open or check?

9. You deal. Everybody else checks. You hold 3 3 2 2 4 — the shortest of the two short pairs. Open or check?

10. Three deals have been passed out. There has been an additional ante after each deal, and there are now twenty-eight chips in the pot. Brill deals, and you are under the gun with J J 6 5 2. You may open for two chips. Open or check?

3

Jackpots

To Open or Not to Open
ANSWERS

1. Check. To open with this holding, *in this position,* would be to abuse the privilege. It is at least an even bet that one of the six players due to take action after you holds a better hand. In any case, if you open under the gun with your anemic J's, anybody after you can embarrass you with a raise. Your hand is unlikely to improve in the draw, and by opening you make it possible for holders of bobtailed straights and four-flushes to come in.

The uninformed player, holding minimum openers, opens in any position. The expert carefully considers position and other strategic factors. See the table of recommended opening requirements for the different positions at Jackpots at the end of this list of answers.

2. Check. Your pair of Q's is too weak to open in this position. Surely, you do not contemplate splitting your Q's and drawing to the inside straight!

3. Open. You will have the option of splitting your J's and drawing one card to your J 10 9 8, if the subsequent action gives you the proper odds. See page 36 for table of odds in the draw.

4. Check. Do not open with two short pairs in this position; do not let the 10's dazzle you. Of the possible 123,552 two pairs, 66,528 are higher than 10's-up, and 44,352 are lower. If any opponent should catch two pairs, they will probably be higher than yours.

5. Open. This is a sound opening hand in any position.

6. Open. Two pairs, J's-up or higher, handled with discretion or imagination or both, will show a profit through the years.

7. Check. Since you catch four of a kind so seldom, and since the hand is so beautiful, you probably cannot bear the thought that the deal may be passed out if you check. But any course other than checking in this situation is, to my mind, timid. You have the opportunity to make a killing with your four of a kind. Consider:

If a player after you can open, and if others come in, you will draw one; then they will read you for a flush or a straight at most, they will suspect you of a bluff, and you will be able to maneuver with lethal effect.

If the deal is passed out, it will mean there would have been no opposition and you will have lost only the ante. By checking, you stand to sacrifice a little or win a lot.

In the biggest pot I have ever won, I checked with this holding. One opponent held a pat A-high flush; another caught a full house. When they had finished whipsawing me, I took my lone raise.

8. Open. It is sound in this position to do so with J's.

9. Open. You probably won't get much action; you may make off with the ante, without a contest.

10. Check. Let us assume that your pair of J's is the best hand before the draw, and that you open. With all those chips beckoning from the table, this crowd, with the exception of Wad and Brill, will march merrily and automatically in. Here is what you may expect:

Potzer, planning to draw two to a three-flush, or something equally ridiculous, will call, saying, "I've got to protect my investment."

Guffy, holding a short pair, will call, saying, "My hand is hideous, but the odds seduce me."

Wad, holding 7 6 3 2 A, will fold, groaning, "I wish this was Lowball."

Mouse, lured by the cheese of an inside straight, will quietly call.

Showbuck, holding a K Q in the same suit, will loudly raise. If he fails to improve in the draw, he will bluff. It won't work. The size of the pot being what it is, somebody will surely "keep him honest."

Brill will fold, unless he holds something much better than minimum openers — or a four-flush or a bobtail — in which event he will put in a scientific raise based on the odds.

Now, with so many more chips on the table, you will probably call. Potzer, nudged by his leprechaun, will raise — and so on.

Individually, each of these characters except Brill will be bucking odds too long for the risk. But if you take them *collectively* — if you add up their chances, such as they are — your J's alone are unlikely to stand up. You must improve, and *the odds are against you.*

And that is why I hope you checked in the first place.

If you opened with four of a kind (question 7), I shall not quarrel with you — you were taking a profit. But if you went wrong with any of the other hands, you were *asking* for "bad luck."

The following are suggested minimum opening requirements at Jackpots and any other natural variation of Five-Card Draw in which the high hand wins and opening is optional:

Number of players who follow *you*	Minimum opening requirements at Jackpots
7	One pair of A's, or
	One pair of K's with a side A, or
	One pair of K's, Q's or J's with a four-flush or bobtail.
	Do not open two short pairs.
6	One pair of K's, or
	One pair of Q's or J's with a four-flush or bobtail.
	Do not open two short pairs.
5	One pair of Q's with a higher side card, or
	One pair of Q's or J's with a four-flush or bobtail.
	Do not open two short pairs.
4	One pair of J's with two higher side cards, or
	One pair of J's with a four-flush or bobtail.
3 (or less) . .	One pair of J's.

An Opponent Opens

QUESTIONS

In each of the following deals, an opponent opens. There is no intervening raise, and it is your turn to act.

1. Wad deals. Mouse checks. Showbuck opens, and you know he habitually opens with minimums in any position.

Brill folds. You hold Q Q 7 5 3. Raise, call, or fold?

2. Mouse deals. Showbuck checks. Brill opens. You hold 8 8 7 7 A. Raise, call, or fold?

3. Showbuck deals. Brill opens. You hold J J 3 3 2. Raise, call, or fold?

4. Wad deals. Showbuck checks. Brill opens. You hold A A A 5 2. Raise or call?

5. Potzer deals. Guffy opens. Wad, Mouse, Showbuck, and Brill fold. You hold 10 10 A 3 2. Raise, call, or fold?

6. Guffy deals. Wad opens. Mouse, Showbuck, and Brill fold. You hold A K Q J 5. Raise, call, or fold?

7. You deal. Potzer opens. The others fold. You hold K Q J 10 6. Raise, call, or fold?

8. Potzer deals. Guffy opens. Wad, Mouse, and Showbuck call. Brill folds. You hold A K Q of Spades and 6 5 of Hearts. Raise, call, or fold?

9. Guffy deals. Wad opens. Mouse, Showbuck, and Brill fold. You hold K J 7 4 2, all Clubs — a flush! Raise or call?

10. Three deals have been passed out. You deal. Potzer opens. It is late in the evening and everyone is at least a little tired. Guffy, Wad and Mouse call. Showbuck fails to put in his usual raise; he calls. Brill folds — you need not worry about trap by him. You hold 9 8 7 5 2, an inside straight. I shall not insult you by asking if you raise. But do you call or fold?

An Opponent Opens

ANSWERS

1. Fold. This is a matter of simple arithmetic. Granted that Showbuck would not hesitate to open under the gun with only one pair of J's, and assuming that he holds no more than one pair, there are two pairs of openers, A's and

K's, higher than your Q's, and there is one pair lower than your Q's. It is very probable he holds more than your Q's. Don't chase: that is a basic principle of winning Poker.

2. Fold. Do not stay with two short pairs in an early position, especially in a group as loose as this. Others will probably come in, and the odds are approximately 11 to 1 you will not improve in the draw. You do not figure to win this pot, so retire.

3. Raise. You probably hold the best hand at this stage, before the draw, but you are unlikely to improve. Protect your hand — try to drive the opposition out. The fewer the stayers, the better your chance to win the pot.

4. Call. This is an opportunity to trap the opposition. Your hand is a probable winner already, and if you improve in the draw, you will hold a near look. Let everybody come in at a low price.

5. Fold. To call would be chasing of the worst kind.

6. Fold. There are only nine chips in the pot and the odds are approximately 11 to 1 you will not catch the straight which is open at only one end.

7. Call. The odds just about balance. The money odds are almost equal to your chance in the draw. There are nine chips in the pot, and you can get in for two: that reduces to 4.5 to 1. The odds are exactly 4.9 to 1 against your catching the straight which is open at both ends, but if you do catch it and win, you will get nearly enough chips to have warranted your call. Throw in your chips with a shrug or any other gesture which may suggest you are chasing. Build up a reputation for occasional looseness.

8. Fold. There are nine chips in the pot. You think of drawing two cards to your three-straight-flush? The odds against catching a flush are 23 to 1; the odds against any other significant improvement are also long. Such a draw

belongs in bisexual Poker, where husbands and wives get together in a group, and folding is considered downright mean.

9. Raise. Too many have already folded. It is too late to trap.

10. Call. This is the rare situation where it is sound to draw to an inside straight — your 9 8 7 5. There have been four antes: the original ante plus the three for the passed-out deals. That made a total of twenty-eight chips in the pot. Potzer, Guffy, Wad, Mouse, and Showbuck have put in two apiece, making a grand total of thirty-eight. You can get in for two — money odds of 19 to 1. The odds against your catching the inside straight are approximately 11 to 1. Get aboard!

I wonder how it would sound if the hero in a western said, *"Hardly ever draw to an inside straight, son."*

This little gimmick of balancing the odds is essential to winning Poker. Whatever the odds against you at your turn to bet, be sure the pot offers equal or better odds. When you play a 5 to 1 shot, be sure you will get five chips for every one you put in, or more than five, and not less than five.

"I don't like to bother my head with such arithmetic," Potzer says.

"Then why do you bother to play this arithmetical game?" Guffy asks.

"Why?" Potzer cocks his head like an inquiring bird. "Why do I play Poker? Because I enjoy it."

Guffy grins. "So do I, but I enjoy it more when I win than when I lose."

An Opponent Raises

QUESTIONS

When the pot has been opened and raised, and it is your turn to act, there is no convenient system for you to follow. You must play the players, as well as the cards. You know more about these players now. Can you profit from this knowledge?

1. Mouse deals. Showbuck opens. Brill raises. You hold A A 8 8 3, known as "the dead man's hand," because, according to western lore, Wild Bill Hickock held it when he was shot. Do you call, raise, or fold?

2. Brill deals. You hold K Q J 10 5, and you check. Potzer opens. Guffy raises. The others fold. Do you now call, raise, or fold?

3. Guffy deals. Wad opens. Mouse calls. Showbuck raises, saying, "Let's see who's really got it." Brill folds. You hold 7 7 5 5 4. Call, raise, or fold?

4. Potzer deals. Guffy opens. Wad calls. Mouse raises. Showbuck raises. Brill raises. You hold A A A 4 2. Call, raise, or fold?

5. You deal. Potzer opens. Guffy, Wad, Mouse, and Showbuck fold. Brill raises. You hold 2 2 2 3 5. Call, raise, or fold?

6. Guffy deals. Wad opens. Mouse and Showbuck fold. Brill raises. You hold K K 9 8 3 with a four-flush. Call, raise, or fold?

7. Potzer deals. Guffy opens — the only sound he makes is with his chips. Wad raises. Mouse, Showbuck, and Brill fold. You hold J J J J 6. Call or raise?

8. Brill deals. You hold 9 8 7 6 5, and you open. The others fold, around to Brill. He raises. Do you call, raise, or fold?

9. Potzer deals. Guffy opens. Wad raises. Mouse, Showbuck, and Brill fold. You hold K K 7 4 3. Call, raise, or fold?

10. Brill deals. You hold K K 4 4 A, and you open. Potzer raises. Guffy, Wad, Mouse, and Showbuck call. Brill folds. Do you call, raise, or drop?

An Opponent Raises

ANSWERS

1. Raise. Showbuck's openers are probably one pair. Brill's raise in his position suggests two pairs: he is trying to protect a hand which is unlikely to improve in the draw.

Your hand, too, is unlikely to improve and is probably the best in the deal at this stage. Try to make it too expensive for the others to come in.

2. Fold. When you picked up your hand, you were hoping somebody would open so that you could draw to your bobtail, but the raise has unbalanced the odds to your disadvantage. The ante, plus the opener's contribution, plus the raise add up to thirteen chips. Potzer will undoubtedly call, as usual, making the total fifteen. It will cost you four chips to stay in, and you will get a fraction less than 4 to 1 money odds. The odds against your catching the straight are a corresponding fraction less than 5 to 1. Moreover, Potzer may reraise. So hang on to your chips.

3. Fold. Wad has solid openers. Mouse's call indicates more. Showbuck's raise may be glandular or may be based on strength. In any case, it does not pay you to play two short pairs now.

4. It's close, but fold. Brill's raise is the tip-off: he wants to build the pot, because he holds a powerful hand. Although it hurts to fold bullet triplets, it will probably hurt more to stay.

5. Raise. This time you have Brill in a pincers. If Potzer should take it into his head to raise, Brill will probably fold, and you should then call.

6. Call, then split your K's and draw one to your four-flush. The odds against your catching the flush are a fraction longer than 4 to 1. While the money odds offered by the pot are a little shorter, you will get a call if you catch and will then show a fair profit.

7. This one, too, is close. A raise is reasonable, but I think a call is better. Remember that Guffy shut off the chatter when he opened, and that Wad's raises usually mean strength. If you raise, you will probably eliminate

Potzer and make Guffy and Wad cautious, so that they may only call. Now, visualize this action after you call:

Potzer mechanically throws in two chips.

Wad barks, "The pot was raised."

Guffy smirks. "Yeah, throw in two more chips."

Potzer obeys.

"Nice boy," Guffy says, as he reraises.

If Wad holds less than a pat hand, he may fold. Even so, you will have replaced him with Potzer, who is more likely to keep on sweetening the pot for you after you draw.

You will draw one, and if anybody reads you for four of a kind, you should break the habit of holding your cards so far out.

8. Raise. Brill is not weak, but your pat hand warrants at least one reraise.

9. Fold. You know Wad's openers are always solid. Since he was under the gun, you should assume he holds at least one pair of A's. Don't chase him; he doesn't chase you.

10. Call. Count the chips in the pot: seven for the ante, plus your two for opening, plus twenty from the five other stayers. The chips total twenty-seven. You can stay for two more. The money odds are 13.5 to 1. The odds against your catching the full house are approximately 11 to 1. How could anyone resist such a supervalue?

Knowing the odds in the draw is a necessity in this and related variations. If you do not already know them, consult the table which follows before the next series of questions.

How Do You Draw

QUESTIONS

Because most Poker players have only a blurred conception of the odds in the draw, and because I think anybody who makes any kind of bet ought to know something about the risk involved, I am including a table of those odds.

If you do not know the odds in the draw, I urge you to study this table before you again sit down to play live Poker. You can memorize these odds in about fifteen minutes. It will pay you to do so; it will give you an enormous advantage over your less informed opposition.

To make the figures easier to memorize, I am using approximations. Thus, 359 to 1 becomes 360 to 1; 4.9 to 1 becomes 5 to 1; 4.2 to 1 becomes 4 to 1. This may disturb some of the purists, as it disturbs me, but most folks do not have our kind of fondness for figures, a fact which was brought home to me ironically a few years ago.

Following publication of an earlier book about Poker, I was invited to address an assemblage of about 150 professional and business men after dinner. "There's lots of Poker players in that bunch, and they'll be glad to get useful information," I was told. I was skeptical, but accepted.

Over 200 showed up. After dinner, the master of ceremonies gave me a build-up in Hollywoodian terms. I stood up and, after a nice burst of applause, asked, "How many of you gentlemen play Poker?"

Virtually everybody raised a hand.

So I went into the arithmetic of a popular variation. There is one brief set of figures I especially like. They are based on some neat computations, are valuable, and to my best knowledge had never appeared in the literature on the game before I published them. Painstakingly, I explained their application.

At this point, I saw some members of the audience beginning to doze and others getting restless.

I switched quickly. I told them an anecdote, and they perked up. For the balance of the lecture, I told nothing

but anecdotes, concluding with one about a flat-chested soprano, and it required some ingenuity to tie that one to Poker. When I sat down, the applause was loud and long.

Before I made my escape, at least a dozen men came over to shake hands. "You really opened my eyes," said one. "Highly instructive," said another. "I learned more about Poker tonight than over the last twenty years," said another. And so it went. Yes, they were serious.

The table of approximate odds in the draw follows.

Hand	Draw	Deception	Improvement	Odds against
One pair	3	None	Four of a kind	360 to 1
			Full house	100 to 1
			Triplets	8 to 1
			Two pairs	5 to 1
			Any	5 to 2
One pair with A kicker	2	Good	Four of a kind	1,100 to 1
			Full house	120 to 1
			Triplets	12 to 1
			Two pairs, A's-up	8 to 1
			Any two pairs	5 to 1
			Any	3 to 1
Two pairs	1	Fair	Full house	11 to 1
Triplets	2	Fair	Four of a kind	23 to 1
			Full house	16 to 1
			Any	9 to 1
Triplets with kicker	1	Excellent	Four of a kind	46 to 1
			Full house	15 to 1
			Any	11 to 1
Four-flush	1	Good	Flush	4 to 1
Bobtail straight	1	Good	Straight	5 to 1
Inside or one-way straight	1	Good	Straight	11 to 1
Four-straight-flush° open at both ends	1	Excellent	Any: straight-flush or straight or flush	2 to 1
Four-straight-flush° open at one end or inside	1	Excellent	Any: straight-flush or straight or flush	3 to 1

°A four-straight-flush occurs, on the average, once in 1,760 five-card hands — so seldom that the breakdown of the different kinds of improvement possible is omitted from the table. Odds against improvement to a straight or flush or straight-flush combined are attractively short. Odds against catching a straight-flush are, by themselves, prohibitive, but this is usually a factor only in a table stakes or pot limit game.

And now try to meet these situations:

1. Potzer opened. The others called around to Brill, and he folded. At the price, you decided to call with Q Q A 6 3.

Now, each of the other stayers draws three. Of course, you keep the Q's. Do you also keep the A kicker?

2. Two deals were passed out; the added antes have made this a big pot. Showbuck opened, and Brill raised. You hold A A Q 7 4, and you refused to be intimidated — you called. The others folded; around to Showbuck; he also called.

Showbuck draws three. Brill draws one. How do you draw?

3. Guffy dealt. Wad, Mouse, Showbuck and Brill checked. You opened with J J A 9 5. Potzer raised, and the others folded. You called.

You must draw before Potzer. How do you draw?

4. You dealt and Potzer opened. The others folded. You raised, properly, with 8 8 5 5 3. Potzer called.

Potzer draws one. How do you draw?

5. You stayed with a Diamond four-flush K 8 7 6 and the Spade 5. Either a flush or a straight should win. Do you draw to the four-flush or to the bobtail?

6. Wad opened. Mouse raised. Showbuck raised. Brill folded. You called with A A A K 4. Potzer and Guffy folded. Wad and Mouse called.

Wad draws one. Mouse stands pat. Showbuck draws one. How do you draw?

7. There are only three stayers. Guffy opened, Wad called, and you raised with 7 7 3 3 K. They called.

Guffy draws three, and so does Wad. You decide to bluff this one through, if necessary. With that in mind, what is your best draw?

8. The pot has been raised and reraised. You stayed with 8 7 6 5 4, a straight which contains a four-flush: the 8 7 5 4 are Spades and the 6 is a Diamond.

Now Guffy, the opener, stands pat. Wad also stands pat. Brill draws one. Do you stand pat or do you draw. If you draw, how?

9. There are only three stayers. Showbuck opened, Brill called, and you called with A A 10 8 2, which is also a four-flush.

Showbuck draws three. Brill draws two. How do you draw?

10. Again, there are only three stayers. Mouse opened, Brill called, and you called with A A K Q J.

Mouse draws two. Brill draws two. How do you draw?

How Do You Draw

ANSWERS

1. Keep your pair of Q's and draw three. With so many stayers, you hope to catch triplets or better. Keeping the A kicker would shorten the odds against your catching two pairs but would lengthen the odds against anything better. Moreover, it is likely that the opener holds a pair of A's. It is unsound here, as in most situations, to hold a kicker with one pair.

2. Keep your pair of A's and the 7: a low-card kicker. Draw two. By doing so, you shorten the odds against catching a second pair, and your two pairs should be enough to win the pot. This sort of draw is sound in small pots. It gains in deception, too.

3. Keep your pair of J's with the A kicker. Draw two.

Potzer probably holds two pairs and probably will not improve in the draw. Your draw shortens the odds against your catching two pairs, A's-up, and they should be enough to win the pot.

4. Obviously, Potzer holds two pairs, and they are probably higher than your 8's-up. Keep your 8's, discard the 5's and the 3, and draw three cards. You hope to catch triplets, or better, or at least a higher second pair. The odds against these catches are much shorter than the odds against your catching a full house with a one-card draw.

5. Draw one to the four-flush. The odds against catching the flush are shorter than those against catching the straight with a one-card draw. Does this mean that flushes outnumber straights? No. Straights outnumber flushes by a substantial margin before and after the draw. But once a four-flush has appeared in the original hand, any one of nine cards will make it a flush, whereas only one of eight cards will make a bobtail a straight.

6. If you catch a full house, it will certainly be good enough to win, so forget about trying to catch four of a kind. Keep your triplet A's and a kicker — draw one. Which kicker? The 3, because it is more probable the opposition holds K's than 3's. By keeping the kicker with your triplets, you shorten the odds against catching a full house, and you may befuddle the opposition. More often than not, it is sound to draw this way to triplets.

7. Stand pat, then bet aggressively. If you are called, your two short pairs may still be winners. Management of two pairs in the original hand is one of the most difficult problems in Jackpots. The hand is usually the best in the deal before the draw, but is unlikely to improve. It indicates vigorous measures when you decide to stay.

8. Competing with two pat hands, your low straight is

inadequate; even if it were a higher straight, it might lose. Break up the straight and draw one to your four-flush. If you catch the flush, bet cautiously.

9. Split your pair of A's and draw one to your four-flush. The odds against catching a flush are appreciably shorter than the odds against improving the pair of A's to triplets or better. If you had reason to believe your hand was the strongest going in, you would keep the pair of A's, but no such belief is warranted here.

10. Keep your pair of A's and draw three. Your chances in this pot are not robust, but try for the triplet A's or better, rather than draw to the one-way straight. The odds against your catching a straight are far too long.

After the Draw

QUESTIONS

Now comes the final round of betting — the action before the showdown. If, in any of the following situations you feel the urge to bluff, remember that this is a game with a moderate limit and that the odds are long against the bluffer. Will that deter some of your opponents from trying to bluff you? Not necessarily.

1. Brill opened under the gun. You called with a four-flush. Potzer and Guffy folded. Wad re-examined his hand and raised. Mouse and Showbuck folded. Brill and you called.

Brill drew two. You drew one and caught the flush, A-high. Wad, trying his best to conceal his rapture, stands pat.

Brill checks. Do you bet or check?

2. Mouse dealt. Showbuck and Brill checked. You opened with one pair of A's. Potzer and Guffy called. The others folded.

You drew three and caught a second pair; you now hold A A 5 5 9. Potzer drew one. Guffy drew three.

You must act first. Do you bet or check?

3. You dealt. The pot was checked around to Brill, who opened. You called with one pair of K's. Everybody else folded.

Brill stood pat. You drew three and caught another K; you now hold K K K 10 2.

Brill bets the limit. Do you raise, call or fold?

4. You dealt. Potzer and Guffy checked. Wad opened. Showbuck called. Brill folded. You called with one pair of A's. The others folded.

Wad drew two. Showbuck drew three. You drew three, and caught another pair. You now hold A A Q Q J.

Wad bets the limit. Showbuck folds, grins at you, and says roguishly, "I'm leaving it to you to keep him honest."

The humor, such as it is, eludes Wad. "I consider that crack highly unethical," he says.

It never occurred to Showbuck that his remark could be anything but harmless. "I was only horsing around," he protests.

"Horse around with somebody else's money," Wad says.

Guffy seizes the opportunity to insert his needle. "The man scoring a knockdown will go to the furthest neutral corner."

Wads turns on him. "Who appointed you referee, blabbermouth?"

Before Guffy can answer, Mouse who is losing raps on the table with a chip. "Come on, gentlemen, play the game."

You are as eager as he is to get on with it. You are not

sure whether Wad's irritability indicates a lock or failure to improve one pair with a kicker. Do you raise, call or fold?

5. This is a big pot. Two deals were passed out and there were three antes. Mouse opened under the gun. Showbuck raised. Brill folded. You, holding triplet A's, raised — a close decision, and the correct one, in my opinion. Potzer called. Guffy raised. Wad called. Mouse folded. Showbuck, who might have driven you out with a reraise, coyly called. You called. So did Potzer, Guffy and Wad.

Showbuck stood pat. I don't know whether you drew one or two; either way, you caught a full house and now hold A A A 4 4. Potzer drew one. Guffy stood pat. Wad drew one.

Showbuck bets the limit. Do you raise or call?

6. You opened under the gun with K K A 5 2. Potzer called. Guffy, Wad and Mouse folded. Showbuck raised with a rumble and a roar. You and Potzer called.

You drew three and failed to improve. Potzer drew three. Showbuck ostentatiously stood pat, and you suspect he holds nothing.

Do you bet or check?

7. Mouse opened under the gun. Showbuck folded. Brill called. You, holding a four-flush, called. The others folded.

Mouse stood pat. Brill drew two. You drew one and now hold a flush.

Mouse bets. Brill calls. Do you raise, call or fold?

8. Mouse dealt. Showbuck and Brill checked. You opened with K K 9 7 2. Potzer called. So did Guffy. Wad folded. Mouse called. Showbuck and Brill folded.

You drew three and failed to improve. Potzer, Guffy and Mouse each drew three.

You check. Potzer bets. Guffy and Mouse call. Do you call or fold?

9. Brill dealt. You checked with K K 10 8 6. Potzer checked. Guffy opened. Wad called. Mouse, Showbuck and Brill folded. You called. Potzer folded.

Guffy drew one. Wad drew one. You drew three and caught another K; you now hold K K K 5 4.

Guffy checks. Wad checks. Do you bet or check?

10. Guffy dealt, and Wad checked. Mouse opened. Showbuck and Brill folded. You raised with Q Q K 3 3. Potzer folded. Guffy, Wad and Mouse called.

Mouse drew three. You drew one and failed to improve. Guffy drew three. Wad drew one.

Mouse bets. Do you raise, call or fold?

After the Draw

ANSWERS

1. It is usually unwise to bet into a pat hand. While your flush is a probable winner, you should check: you have nothing to gain by betting.

If you bet, you will merely advertise a holding better than a straight. With less than a full house, Wad will call; with a full house, he will probably raise. And remember that Brill drew two, probably to triplets — he may be trapping.

After you check, Wad will undoubtedly bet. You will have lost nothing except the opportunity to get a line, gratis, on Brill's holding.

2. Check. It is usually unwise to bet into one-card draws, unless you hold a high straight or better; even then you lose little if anything by checking.

3. Call. Brill is astute enough, in situations such as this, to stand pat with two pairs. He may be bluffing. If he holds an authentic pat hand, you are stuck.

4. Don't low-rate Wad's reasoning in practical matters or his self control where money is involved. If he had a weak hand, he would have waited until after the showdown to blast Showbuck. He certainly holds triplets, or more, and you should fold. Do you want to invest a few chips so that you may look at his hand to confirm your judgment for future reference? In that case, I have no quarrel with your call; after all, you have not known Wad as long as I have.

5. If you drew two, any bet by you now will amount to an assertion that you hold a full house, so you may as well raise. If you drew one, you are in a better strategic position: you can trap with a call. That way, you will invite a raise and you can reraise when it is again your turn to bet.

6. You have more to fear from Potzer than from Showbuck, so bet. Potzer, anticipating a raise from Showbuck, may fold a hand which is better than yours. Try to squeeze Potzer out of there.

7. Fold. Brill, who drew two, probably to triplets, holds a full house or four of a kind — he is trapping you.

8. Even though you can stay for little, fold. You are surely beaten. Cheap calls in such situations can add up to substantial amounts over the course of a year.

9. Although you hold what is probably the best hand, check. You have nothing to gain by betting into Guffy's one-card draw.

10. Fold. Mouse, the timid player, undoubtedly improved his high opening pair. At best, you are now second, and more probably third. There is no payoff for these positions in Poker.

4

Lowball

QUESTIONS

In this simple variation of Draw, the idea is to catch the lowest hand possible, to avoid a pair or anything higher. Flushes and straights are not recognized; an A counts as a 1; the lowest hand is 5 4 3 2 A, called a "Wheel" or "Bicycle." One pair of A's ranks below one pair of Deuces.

Anybody, in his turn, may open on anything.

At the usual Lowball game, you will encounter some of the most inept opposition: players trying to escape what they consider their bad luck at variations in which the high hand wins. You may encounter, also, one or two sharpshooting experts.

Lowball is popular in California, where it is often played with the wild Joker.

The group you have just joined plays Lowball on occasion, without the Joker. Potzer, the dealer, has just announced it.

"Great game," Guffy says. Secretly, he dislikes it, but he finds it politic to humor Potzer.

"Lowball is for the birds," Wad says.

"So I'm a bird." Potzer riffles the deck. "Yep, Lowball."

Brill, saying nothing, prepares to play the role of hawk.

1. Potzer deals. Everybody checks around to you. You hold Q J 3 2 A. Do you open or check?

2. Guffy deals. Mouse checks. Wad opens. Showbuck calls. Brill folds. You hold K 6 6 4 2. Do you raise, call, or fold?

3. Mouse deals. Wad, Showbuck, and Brill check. You hold 9 7 6 5 3. Do you open or check?

4. Wad deals. Showbuck opens. Brill folds. You hold 8 7 6 5 A. Do you raise, call, or fold?

5. Showbuck deals. Brill opens. You hold 6 5 4 3 A. Do you raise or call?

6. Brill deals. You hold Q 8 6 4 A. Do you open or check?

7. You deal. Potzer opens. Guffy folds. Wad and Mouse call. Showbuck folds. Brill calls. You hold 7 5 4 3 2. Do you raise or call?

8. Potzer deals. Guffy opens. Wad folds. Mouse calls. Showbuck raises. Brill calls. You hold 9 6 4 2 A and you call. Potzer folds. Guffy and Mouse call.

Guffy draws one. Mouse draws one. Showbuck stands pat. Brill draws one. What do you do?

9. Guffy deals. Wad and Mouse check. Showbuck opens. Brill folds. You hold K 7 6 4 2 and you call. The others fold.

Showbuck draws one. You discard the K and draw one:

you catch a J and now hold J 7 6 4 2. Showbuck bets the limit. Do you raise, call, or fold?

10. Wad deals. Wad and Mouse check. Showbuck opens. Brill folds. You hold Q 8 5 4 A and you call. The others fold.

Showbuck draws two. You discard the Q, draw one, and catch an A; you now hold 8 5 4 A A.

Showbuck bets two chips. Do you raise, call, or fold?

ANSWERS

1. Check. If anybody else opens, fold when the betting again reaches you. At Lowball, you should draw no more than one, and then only to a hand which can become an 8-high or lower. When you hold three low cards and draw two, the odds are 6 to 1 against your catching an 8-high or lower. The only time the pot offers money odds to balance the odds in a two-card draw is when many stay, and that means: (*a*) there are many low cards held by your opponents, lengthening the odds against you, or (*b*) your opponents are nutty, and you can profit by staying sane.

2. Fold. Here again, you would have to draw two.

3. Open. Plan to stand pat, check, and call, unless subsequent action indicates you are beaten. A 9-high wins more often than not.

4. Raise. Your hand is probably the best before the draw, and you plan to stand pat. However, it is one of the weakest 8-highs possible, and if several stay, you may be outcaught. Protect your hand, as you would holding two pairs at Jackpots: try to drive out the opposition.

5. Call. While your hand is not a lock, it is an almost certain winner, so let the opposition come in.

6. Open, with a view to discarding the Q and drawing one. The odds against your catching an 8-high are only 2 to 1.

7. Raise. There are already plenty of stayers, and your hand is a probable winner. Make them pay.

8. Against the pat hand and three one-card draws, your 9-high is probably futile. Try to improve. Painful though it may be, discard the 9 and draw one.

9. Count the chips. The pot offers better than 5 to 1 money odds. The odds against Showbuck's having caught a higher hand than yours are 2 to 1. Showbuck is a frequent bluffer. Call.

10. When a player draws two, the probability of catching a pair is approximately 1 in 3 and the odds against it are only 2 to 1. Here again, the pot offers longer money odds. Since your pair is the lowest possible, call.

The hands with which it is sound to stay at Lowball are:

9-high and lower, unpaired	129,024
Four unpaired cards below 9, one above	286,720
Five cards below 9, one paired	107,520
Total	523,264

The odds against starting with such a hand are approximately 4 to 1. Staying in more than one of five deals on the average constitutes loose play and is costly.

Where Lowball is played with the wild Joker, there is a slight increase in the number of playable hands. The odds in the draw are shortened when one holds three low cards with the Joker, and such a hand should be played optimistically. A temptation to be resisted is to stay with two low cards and the Joker; the two-card draw remains unsound,

because the odds against catching an 8-high or lower are
not sufficiently shortened.

If you enjoy both Lowball and Jackpots, here is a variation which speeds up the game by combining them and
tends to eliminate passed-out deals: "Jackson", also called
"Jacks-and-Back." Each deal starts out as Jackpots. If nobody opens with one pair of Jacks or better, the deal becomes Lowball; then anybody, in his turn, may open with
anything. A low hand gives you something to hope for.

At Jackson, in an early position, should you open with
a hand such as J J Q 9 7, before the deal becomes Lowball? The answer is no. Let the deal become Lowball and
then, if anybody opens, you fold. The reason for this is that
it is wiser to sacrifice the ante than to trap yourself with
an unsound opening bet.

5

Five-Card Stud

Five-Card Stud was invented about 1870 and is the simplest form of Stud. It can accommodate at least ten players, and that is its sole merit at a low or moderate limit. When played rationally, Five-Card Stud becomes exceedingly tight, with few stayers. To be exciting, it must be played without a limit, or for table stakes, or for pot limit, or with a bet-the-raise proviso.

Despite the dullness of Five-Card, this group occasionally plays it, at the following stakes: one chip ante by each player; two chip limit until a pair shows or the last card is dealt; then the limit is increased to four chips.

At the option of the dealer, this variation may be introduced: *a four-flush beats one pair*. It is a logical variation, because a four-flush in five cards occurs almost as seldom as do two pairs.

Wad, who is about to deal, has just announced Five-Card Stud. He is winning, and he thinks it will help conserve his chips.

At this point, another regular in the group appears behind a squat pipe with a big bowl: Pundit. "I'm sorry I'm a little late tonight," he says, "but it's my thirtieth wedding anniversary."

"I know how it is," Guffy says. "I'm kind of sentimental myself."

Ignoring Guffy, Pundit accepts the congratulations of the others, along with banalities on the subject of matrimony. The principal theme is the effect of age on sexual prowess. Smiling in a manner intended to be enigmatic, Pundit sits down between Wad and Mouse and buys a stack of chips.

"Get it up," Wad says. "I mean your ante."

"Thanks for the clarification." Pundit antes. "What are we playing?"

"I'm sorry, I'm a little late tonight, but it's my 30th wedding anniversary"

"Five-Card Stud." Wad passes the deck to Guffy to cut.

"A four-flush beats one pair?" Potzer asks hopefully. He wants an added excuse for staying.

"Yeah, provided it contains a higher pair." Wad begins dealing.

"Nothing wild except the players," Pundit says. The cornball pun elicits a few snickers. Pundit thinks he has been witty.

1. Wad deals. The open cards:

Pundit	9
Mouse	Q
Showbuck	A
Brill	5
You	K
Potzer	J
Guffy	6
Wad	3

Showbuck bets. Brill folds. You have a Q in the hole. Do you raise, call, or fold?

2. Pundit deals. The open cards:

Mouse	7
Showbuck	10
Brill	K
You	2
Potzer	Q
Guffy	J
Wad	8
Pundit	Q

Brill checks. You have another 2 in the hole, a wired pair. Do you open or check?

3. Mouse deals. The open cards:

> Showbuck .... A
> Brill .... J
> You 2
> Potzer .... Q
> Guffy 8
> Wad .... K
> Pundit 10
> Mouse .... K

Showbuck checks. Brill bets. Again, you have another 2, a wired pair. Do you raise, call, or fold?

4. Showbuck deals. The open cards:

> Brill .... K
> You 8
> Potzer .... A
> Guffy .... J
> Wad 10
> Pundit 6
> Mouse 9
> Showbuck 3

Potzer opens. Guffy calls. Wad folds. Pundit calls. Mouse folds. Showbuck calls. Brill calls. That makes a total of five stayers ahead of you. You have another 8 in the hole, a wired pair. Do you raise, call, or fold?

5. Brill deals. The open cards:

> You .... Q
> Potzer 4
> Guffy 9
> Wad .... J

Pundit 7
Mouse .... Q
Showbuck 7
Brill 4

You have a 9 in the hole. You must act first. Do you open or check?

6. You deal. The open cards:

Potzer .... A
Guffy 6
Wad .... Q
Pundit 9
Mouse .... K
Showbuck 2
Brill .... J
You 10

Potzer opens. Guffy and Wad fold. Pundit calls. Mouse and Showbuck fold. Brill raises. You have another 10 in the hole, a wired pair. Do you raise, call, or fold?

7. Potzer deals. "Four-flush beats a pair," he chirps. "To beat or not to beat, that is the question," Guffy says. "Ugh!" Pundit goes. He sneers at all puns but his own, by invention or adoption.
The open cards:

Guffy .... K
Wad 7
Pundit .... Q
Mouse 10
Showbuck 5
Brill 8
You .... J
Potzer .... Q

Guffy hesitates. With a sidewise look at him, Wad growls, "Whadda you do, Shakespeare?" Guffy opens. Wad calls. Pundit calls. Mouse, Showbuck, and Brill fold. You have a 9 in the hole — your J and 9 are both Hearts and not another Heart shows. Do you raise, call, or fold?

8. Guffy deals. "Let's try that again," he says. "Four-flush beats a pair." Wad, showing an A, opens. Pundit, showing a 7, and you with a wired pair of 6's are the only other stayers. Guffy deals the third card. The open cards:

Wad .... A 4
Pundit .... 7, 9, both Spades
You .... 6 J

Wad bets. Pundit raises. You remember that no other open Spade has been dealt. Is Pundit raising on a pair? A three-flush? Is it a batty bluff? Do you raise, call, or fold?

9. Wad deals. "Back to normal," he says. "None of that four-flush nonsense." You catch wired K's. No A shows, and you open. The only other stayers are Potzer, who shows a 2, and Pundit, who shows a Q.

The third card pairs Potzer's 2's, and he bets. Pundit, who has caught a 6, folds. You have caught an A. Potzer checks. You bet four chips, and he calls.

The fourth card is dealt, and Potzer shows 2 2 2.

Your fourth card is another A, and with a K in the hole you show K A A.

You remember that no other open 2's, K's, or A's have been dealt.

Potzer bets four chips. Do you call or fold?

10. Pundit deals. You again catch a wired pair, Q's. Your open Q is high and you bet. Everybody except Brill folds; he shows a J and calls.

The third and fourth cards do not visibly improve either hand. Your Q remains high, and you bet two chips each time. Brill calls and hangs on grimly.

The fifth card is dealt, and Brill catches an A. He shows J 10 4 A, and no emotion as he bets.

You show K 3 9 8.

There is no tell whatsoever in Brill's manner. Do you raise, call, or fold?

---

1. An established principle in this variation is: When the first two cards have been dealt, fold unless you hold a wired pair or unless your hole card is higher than any opposing open card. There are two exceptions: (*a*) If your hole card matches the highest opposing open card, and your open card is a 10 or higher, you may stay. (*b*) If your open card beats the board, and if your hole card is a 10 or higher, you may stay.

In this deal, your hand meets none of the foregoing requirements, so you should fold.

2. Open. If four or more of your opponents stay, and if one of them raises, fold. If they stay without raising, and if your third card fails to improve your hand, fold on the next round. Against four stayers, do not pay to play any pair lower than 8's.

Against five stayers, do not pay to play any pair lower than 9's. The reason is that you probably will fail to improve, and one of the stayers will probably catch a higher hand.

3. Raise. At this stage you probably hold the highest hand, but if several opponents stay, you will probably be outcaught. Try to drive them out.

4. Fold. Five opponents are staying, and your 8's probably will not stand up.

5. Check. The principle is: When the first two cards have been dealt, do not stay if (a) yours are unpaired, and each is lower than a 10, or (b) yours are unpaired, one is a Q or J, and the other is lower than a 10.

6. Read Brill for wired J's. Fold. Do not chase.

7. Fold. Your two-flush is a siren with a cracked voice. Even though none of your opponents shows a card in your suit, the odds against your catching a four-flush in five cards are approximately 10 to 1. The pot does not offer money odds to compensate. If you stay, the danger is that you will catch a pair and be suckered in all the way.

8. Most probably Pundit is raising on a three-flush. If that is the case, if he is not already paired, the odds against his improving to a flush, four-flush, or higher pair than yours are very short — less than 2 to 1. You must also beat Potzer. Of course, you can also improve, but the odds are long against it. For you, this is a raise-or-fold situation. To raise would be foolhardy. Fold. If Pundit is bluffing, let yourself be bluffed.

9. Your two pairs, A's and K's, are like a pretty but untrained girl competing in a beauty contest with a professional model. In this situation, you would not stay with an inside or one-way straight, would you? The odds against the only possible improvement, to a full house, are just as long: only one of four cards can help you. Even disregarding the possibility that Potzer holds four 2's, those odds are too long. Fold.

10. This is the sort of situation which could produce a

crescendo but for the muting limit. For that matter, Five-Card Stud at any limit gives a generous measure of comfort to the player who is incapable of improvisation, not that Brill is in that category. He is simply adjusting his tactics to the stakes and to you.

You know that Brill's hole card must be an A, K, Q, or J, or else he would not have stayed at all. Rule out the J, because with wired J's, he would probably have put in a raise to test you at an earlier stage. Simple arithmetic makes it probable that his hole card is an A or a K, rather than a Q: the outstanding A's and K's total eight; the outstanding Q's total only too. Between the A's and the K's, it is an even bet, arithmetically. But the problem lies more in the realm of psychology than arithmetic.

If Brill's hole card is an A, he has a lock, and he knows it, but you cannot be sure.

In a table-stakes game, holding less than an A in the hole, he would be in an excellent bluffing position, one which occurs frequently in this variation. He could tap for several hundred chips, unbalancing the odds, and forcing a difficult choice upon you.

Here, at the four chip limit, a bluff is virtually futile and that is the point! Because Brill respects your game, because he credits you with imagination, he may have decided to bluff. He would not dream of trying to bluff Potzer, Pundit, or Showbuck. Potzer would call without pausing to think. Pundit would think, confuse himself all the more, go into a trance, and call with the *elan* of a zombie. Showbuck would call automatically to maintain status, to remind everybody that there is more whence this money comes. He might even raise for emphasis.

What do you do? Since you can beat what you can see, I presume you call. In these circumstances, so would I.

What would I do in a table-stakes game? I would not let this problem develop. After the fourth card had been dealt, and with the odds solidly in my favor, I would try to tap my opponent out; I would bet the maximum. If he folded, I would take the moderate profit and be satisfied. If he called, he would be bucking the odds, hoping to out-catch me, and I adore such opponents. For every pot they win from me, they sweeten several which I win.

6

Six-Card Stud

The First Round

QUESTIONS

Six-Card Stud, also called "Klondike" and "Keeno," provides a fine balance between the closed and the open cards. More complicated, with the ratio of obvious locks reduced, it encourages more action than the five-card variation.

In this group, as in most, Six-Card Stud is dealt as follows: Two cards in the hole and one open, followed by the first round of betting. To each stayer, three more open cards are available, one at a time, and each is followed by a round of betting.

The stakes in this group are: one chip ante by each player; two chip limit until a pair shows or the fifth card is dealt; then the limit is increased to four chips.

"Nothing wild but the players," Pundit says.

1. Potzer deals. You hold the only open A and J 8 in the hole. Do you bet or check?

2. Guffy deals. The open cards:

Wad 2
Pundit 8
Mouse .... K
Showbuck .... Q
Brill 9
You 6
Potzer .... J
Guffy .... K

Mouse bets. Showbuck calls. Brill folds. Your hole cards are 4 4. Do you raise, call, or fold?

3. Wad deals. The open cards:

Pundit 2
Mouse .... A
Showbuck .... Q
Brill .... A
You .... J
Potzer 8
Guffy 4
Wad 10

Mouse bets. Showbuck calls. Brill folds. Your hole cards are 3 3. Do you raise, call, or fold?

4. Pundit deals. The open cards:

Mouse 7
Showbuck 5
Brill .... K
You 6

Potzer .... Q
Guffy 10
Wad .... J
Pundit 4

Brill bets. Your hole cards are A A. Do you raise or call?

5. Mouse deals. The open cards:

Showbuck .... K
Brill 10
You .... Q
Potzer 9
Guffy 3
Wad .... J
Pundit 8
Mouse .... K

Showbuck bets. Brill calls. Your hole cards are Q 7. Do you raise, call, or fold?

6. Showbuck deals. The open cards:

Brill 2
You 10
Potzer .... A
Guffy 7
Wad .... K
Pundit 6
Mouse 3
Showbuck 5

Potzer bets. Guffy and Wad fold. Pundit calls. Mouse, Showbuck and Brill fold. Your hole cards are 9 8, in different suits; you hold a three-straight. Do you raise, call, or fold?

7. Brill deals. Your open card is a Q, which beats the board. Your hole cards are 7 3, in the same suit; you hold a three-flush. Do you bet or check?

8. You deal. Potzer's open K beats the board, and he bets. The others fold around to Brill; he shows a J and he raises. You show a 7. Your hole cards are 6 5, in the same suit; you hold a three-straight-flush. Do you raise, call, or fold?

9. Potzer deals. Brill shows an A and he bets. You hold wired triplet 8's. Do you raise or call?

10. Guffy deals. You show a K, and it beats the board; your hole cards are A Q in different suits. Nobody else shows a card higher than a 10. Do you bet or check?

The First Round

ANSWERS

1. When the first three cards have been dealt, a pair occurs once in six hands on the average. You have seven opponents, and it is probable that at least one of them holds a pair. Although you beat the board, check; do not expose yourself to a raise or a trap call.

2. This is a raise-or-fold situation, and the prudent course is to fold. It is a poor risk to stay with a pair lower than 7's, unless your side card is a J or higher, because you want to be able to draw to a high card as well as the pair.

3. Raise. Your side card warrants your staying, and your low pair needs protection. Your raise should discourage some of the opposition. Morever, the stayers may read you for a pair of J's.

4. You are far out in front, unless somebody holds trip-

lets, and that is unlikely — wired triplets at this stage appear only once in 425 hands on the average. Let the opposition waltz in. Plan to raise at a later stage, when you catch a lower open card. If somebody raises during the first round, you should reraise. Right now, call.

5. Do you smell the herring? Brill is trapping, probably with a high pair in the hole, and possibly with triplet 10's. Still, your Q's are too good to fold. Call and await developments.

6. Do you think you'll catch a Q J, or a J 7, or a 7 6 — a straight — in the remaining cards? I hope you drop the idea and fold now.

An accurate table of the odds against improving the different kinds of three-straights to straights, in the Stud variations dealt this way, would involve intricate probability calculations and would be exceedingly cumbersome. It would have to take into consideration various numbers of players, because every additional open card affects the odds. It would have to include various combinations of cards which could be useful to you but are open elsewhere. You don't need it. All you need is this pertinent fact: When you start with a three-straight open at both ends, the odds against your catching a straight in the remaining three average approximately 10 to 1. Shorten those odds a little, and the risk is still much too great.

It is *never* sound to stay with a low three-straight. On occasion, when the cost is not too high, you may find it profitable to stay with a Q J 10, or a K Q J. Please observe that, for the purpose of catching a straight, a Q J 10 is better, because if you catch a K you are still open at both ends, whereas, if you catch an A to a K Q J, you are open at only one end.

Most devotees of Six-Card Stud automatically stay with

three-straights; experience teaches them nothing. Take their chips. Hold on to yours.

7. Check. If anybody else opens, you should fold. The odds against improving a three-flush to a flush are, on the average, slightly longer than the odds against improving a three-straight to a straight. The fact that a flush outranks a straight has no bearing on the matter; either will usually win the pot, and each occurs too seldom for the risk.

"Aaa, how tight can you get!" Pundit says. "It isn't a question of odds. It's a question of what fate has in store for you."

Ten times out of eleven, fate has a painful kick in store for him. Fate plays no favorites. The real question is: Why invite the kick?

8. Call. Because of the combined opportunities for improvement, a three-straight-flush is playable. The odds are cut approximately in half.

9. Let the latch hang free and invite everybody with a call. Register reluctance, but don't overdo it. You figure to win this pot, even if you fail to improve. What if Potzer, staying with a 5 3 2, catches a 6 and then a 4? If he brings off this coup, he will itch to give the chips back to you. Do not deprive him of his enjoyment.

10. Check. If an opponent opens, and if there are no intervening raises, you may stay if you feel so inclined, to show your sporting spirit.

The Subsequent Action

QUESTIONS

Again and again, the subsequent action demonstrates that a low down payment for staying on the first round can lead to ruinous maintenance costs.

1. Showbuck showed an A and he bet. You, with a K open and a K in the hole, are the only other stayer.

Now, Showbuck shows A A. You catch a Q. He bets four chips, and that makes a total of sixteen in the pot. Do you call or fold?

2. Potzer, Guffy, Pundit, Mouse, and Showbuck have stayed. So have you with an open K and a pair of 4's in the hole. The fourth card is dealt. The open cards:

Potzer	A 2
Guffy	Q 9
Pundit	8 7
Mouse	J 5
Showbuck	7 3
You	K 6

Potzer bets and the others call. You can stay for only two more chips. Do you? Do you raise? Or do you kiss your 4's good-bye.

3. Let us suppose that, because most of the open cards on the first round were low and there were no raises, you stayed with an open 10 and a Q J in the hole.

You catch a 9. Brill shows a pair of 6's and he bets. Mouse's and Pundit's open cards are not pairs, not cards you need for your straight. Do you raise, call or fold?

4. You stayed with the Diamond J 10 9, and you now catch the Spade Q. The other stayers and their open cards:

Potzer	9 9
Guffy	8 K

Pundit .... K 2
Mouse .... A 4

Potzer bets four chips. Guffy says, "I'll give that a little bunt," and he raises. Pundit folds. Mouse calls. With your bobtail, do you raise, call or fold?

5. Brill showed an A, and he bet. You, with a J open and a J 10 in the hole, raised. Potzer showed a K, and he called. Guffy, Wad, Pundit, and Mouse folded low cards. Showbuck showed a 6 and he called. Brill, after a moment's reflection, called.

The fourth card is dealt, and the stayers show:

Potzer .... K K
Showbuck ...: 6 5
Brill .... A 7
You .... J Q

Potzer bets four chips. Showbuck calls. Brill folds. You hold a three-straight, as well as the pair of J's. Do you raise, call or fold?

6. You stayed with the Club 10 9 8, and you caught the Club J. From the start the action has been furious — Guffy, Wad, Pundit, and Brill are still in there. The fifth card is dealt, and the stayers show:

Guffy .... A A A
Wad .... J 8 J
Pundit .... K 3 2, all Hearts
Brill 6 4 6
You .... 8 J Q

Your Q is a Spade; you hold a straight, along with your Club four-straight-flush, and not many Clubs show. The open 8's are not Clubs, so you can still catch the lock at either end.

Guffy says, "With business so good, I see no reason for cutting prices," and he bets four chips.

"It takes brains to play this game?" Wad sneers at Guffy, and disgustedly folds. Obviously, Wad has decided not to chase with his triplet J's.

"I'd rather be lucky than brainy." Guffy grins back at Wad, then directs his gaze to Pundit. "Whadda you do?"

"I raise. That's what I do." Pundit throws in eight chips. Brill calls.

What do you do?

7. Potzer, Mouse, Showbuck, and you have stayed to the end. The open cards:

Potzer	A 3 A 5
Mouse	9 8 8 2
Showbuck	K 4 6 3
You	J 7 7 2

Potzer bets. Mouse and Showbuck call. You have J 10 in the hole. Raise, call or fold?

8. Pundit and you are the only stayers. He shows J 10 9 8 in different suits. You show K 3 9 4 in different suits and you have a pair of 6's in the hole. You know Pundit is unpredictable, and you can beat what you can see. Do you call or fold?

9. Potzer, the dealer, announced, "Royalties for four of a kind or better — two chips a man." Brill showed an A and bet. You, with wired triplet 5's, called, but you lured in only Guffy. Guffy caught an open pair of J's on the fourth card, and he quietly checked. Brill checked. You caught a useless low card; you bet, Guffy called, and Brill folded.

Potzer deals the fifth card, and Guffy shows triplet J's. You fail to improve. Perhaps you wish you had bet more vigorously at an earlier stage. Meanwhile, Guffy reads you well. Betting four chips, he asks you, "Gonna go for the royalties?" Do you call or fold?

10. The sixth card has been dealt, and you hold a straight, with an open K which beats the board. Wad, the only remaining stayer, shows four Spades. You remember that seven Spades showed in the folded hands. That leaves only two Spades, and the odds are long against Wad's having either of them in the hole. Still . . . he could have the flush. Do you bet or check?

The Subsequent Action
ANSWERS

1. Fold. In this situation, your K's are no better than any lower pair. Don't chase.

2. A vital probability figure applies here. When four cards have been dealt, a pair occurs in three hands of ten on the average. That reduces to approximately one in three. Competing with five stayers, you should assume that at least one of them holds a pair, and it is probably higher than yours. Another consideration is that in this loose game, you can count on several stayers all the way. If you are not already beaten, one of them will probably improve and you probably won't. Fold now.

3. Call. The cards you need for your straight are live, and you may pair one or two of your high cards. The odds are short against your catching a winning hand.

4. You need a K or an 8 for your straight. Two K's and two 8's show. You have only a four-card chance which is as bad as an inside straight. With only two more cards

available, give up on the remote flush chance: fold.

5. The odds against your catching your straight have become prohibitive, and surely you don't want to buck K's with J's; save chips and fold.

6. You are sure Guffy holds no more than the triplet A's; he is chattering. Pundit presents you with a problem: Does he hold a flush, or has Guffy goaded him into a foolish raise on a four-flush? It does not matter. Brill is the man who worries you. With less than a full house, he would have folded. With a full house, he would have raised. He holds four 6's and is trying to sucker you in. Even if you credit him with only a full house, you should fold, if you are playing for profit. The odds against your catching the straight-flush are too long. But a straight-flush is so glamorous! If you are playing for fun, you probably call. At these stakes, so might I.

7. Potzer may hold no more than the pair of A's, and Mouse no more than two short pairs, and Showbuck ditto, but the probability is that at least one of them beats you. Fold.

8. Members of the keep-them-honest school always call in such situations. I think you should fold. Pundit may not hold the straight, but in that case he almost certainly holds at least one pair higher than yours.

The identical situation came up recently in one of my games. After I had folded, my opponent gleefully turned up two worthless hole cards. The others, too, were happy about it. Flattering, but no compensation for the twenty chips I had given up. What more than compensated was that, over the course of the evening, I saved about fifty chips by folding in comparable situations. Fifty minus twenty equals thirty — not a bad over-all profit.

9. Fold, and forget about the possible royalties; the odds

against your catching the case 5 are too long. Don't chase
Guffy's triplet J's. He may already hold a full house. If he
does not already hold it, he could catch it with no more
difficulty than you could catch yours, and if you both
caught, his would be higher.

10. Although some skilled players will give me an argument about this one, my recommendation is that you bet —
yes, bet into a hand which can, conceivably, beat yours.

Wad probably holds two pairs or one pair. In that event,
if you check, so will he, and he will then get a free look
at your hole cards. If you bet, he will call, and your additional profit will be four chips.

If, as is improbable, Wad holds a flush, your bet gives
him the chance to put in a sure-thing raise, which should
be your cue to fold, unless you appraise it as his semi-
annual bluff. There is an element of risk in betting, but
weighing all considerations, betting is indicated. Repeating
this procedure in similar situations, you will win about forty
chips for every four you lose.

7

Seven-Card Stud

The First Round
QUESTIONS

"Down the River" is an alternate name for this variation which often builds big pots. It is usually dealt as follows: Two cards in the hole and one open, followed by the first round of betting. To each stayer, three more open cards and a final hole card are available, one at a time, and each is followed by a round of betting.

A complete hand consists of three hole cards and four open cards. That added hole card makes an enormous difference. Big hands are common, there is an added round of betting, and there are more traps. It is possible, for example, to hold four of a kind without an open pair. An open bobtail in an opponent's hand may steer your thoughts away from a concealed full house; the player who shows Q J 10 9 may hold Q Q J in the hole.

The stakes at Seven-Card Stud in this group are one chip ante by each player; two chip limit until a pair shows or the sixth card is dealt; then the limit is increased to four chips.

As Brill shuffles, Pundit says, "Nothing wild but the players."

Guffy reflectively rubs his chin. "Haven't I heard that one before?"

"Your cracks aren't always so original either," Pundit answers.

Wad, who has just finished second in a big pot, growls, "The both of you give me a pain in the neck."

"We add up to two pains." Guffy holds up two fingers.

"Never mind teaching me arithmetic." Wad glares at Guffy.

Pundit mutters something unintelligible.

Certain that he has needled Pundit and Wad to the point where advantage will accrue to him, Guffy takes aim at Brill. "What choice dish have you concocted for us, professor?"

"Skip the titles, chum." Brill points to the ante. "You will have the privilege of asking questions after you have met your initial obligation."

Guffy hesitatingly reaches for one of his chips. "I thought I did ante."

"*You did not!*" Pundit and Wad yip simultaneously.

Mouse, who has often been Guffy's target, chuckles. "Our silent friend fudges about a hundred bucks a year that way."

"So I made a mistake." Guffy, now in the defensive, antes. He should have known better than to tangle with Brill.

"Down the River, gentlemen." Brill starts dealing.

"Nothing wild but the players," Pundit says. It is a declaration of independence.

1. You show an A and have 2 2 in the hole. Bet or check?

2. You deal. Showbuck's open K beats the board and he bets. Brill folds a J. You show a 5 and have a Q 5 in the hole. Raise, call, or fold?

3. Potzer deals. Brill shows the only A and he bets. You show a J; you have a 10 9 in different suits in the hole. None of the cards you need for your straight shows. Do you raise, call, or fold?

4. Guffy deals. Your open K beats the board; you have a Q J in different suits in the hole. None of the cards you need for your straight shows. Bet or check?

5. Wad deals. He shows an A and he bets. Pundit shows a J and he calls. Mouse, Showbuck, and Brill fold low cards. You show the Heart Q and have the Heart 8 6 in the hole. Only one Heart shows elsewhere. Do you raise, call, or fold?

6. Pundit deals. The open cards:

Mouse	9
Showbuck	7
Brill	K
You	7
Potzer	3
Guffy	8
Wad	10
Pundit	4

Brill bets. You have a pair of 5's in the hole. Raise or call?

7. Mouse deals. The open cards:

Showbuck	4
Brill	7
You	4 of Spades

Potzer	A
Guffy	2
Wad	A
Pundit	J
Mouse	9

Potzer bets. Guffy and Wad fold. Mouse calls. Showbuck and Brill fold. You have the 6 5 of Spades in the hole; you hold a three-straight-flush. Do you raise, call, or fold?

8. Showbuck deals himself the only open A and he bets. Brill folds a 5. You show a 3 and you have a pair of A's in the hole. Raise or call?

9. Brill deals. The open cards:

You	9
Potzer	8
Guffy	5
Wad	5
Pundit	2
Mouse	7
Showbuck	6
Brill	3

Not a picture shows and your 9 beats the board. You have two more 9's in the hole, wired triplets. Do you bet or check?

10. You deal. The open cards:

Potzer	Q
Guffy	A
Wad	4
Pundit	4
Mouse	8

Showbuck .... J
Brill 10
You 4

Guffy bets. Wad and Pundit fold. Mouse calls. Showbuck and Brill fold. You have a Q 4 in the hole. Raise, call, or fold?

The First Round

ANSWERS

1. Bet. Usually, it is sound on the first round to stay with any closed pair. Here, your A is a strong side card. Two pairs, A's-up, will show a profit over the long pull.

2. Fold. Do not stay with a split pair lower than 6's, primarily because of the lack of concealment.

3. Call. Unless too many of the cards you need show, it is a fair risk to stay with a J 10 9, or a Q J 10.

4. It's close, but the odds against your catching the straight are a little too long. Fold. Observe that if you catch an A you will be open at only one end.

5. Fold. Do not stay with a three-flush which lacks a J 10, or two higher cards, or an A in the hole. The odds against your catching the flush are too long, and you want high cards to pair as an alternative.

6. Raise, because your low pair needs protection, and the trash shown by the opposition indicates you can drive out some of it. If you feel pessimistic and prefer to fold, you may be proved right, but a call is clearly wrong.

7. Call. Stay on the first round with any three-straight-flush.

8. Raise. You don't expect to catch the case A. Your most

probable improvement is to two pairs, and you don't want many stayers.

9. If you check, you run the risk that the deal may be passed out, but that risk is very slight. Observe that Potzer beats all the others as far as he can see, and when have you known him to check in such a situation? Moreover, there are undoubtedly plenty of high hole cards around the table. If Potzer checks, somebody else will probably try to steal the ante by betting. So check, with a view to betting vigorously during later rounds.

10. Fold. Your 4's are dead, and there isn't much life in your Q.

The Subsequent Action

QUESTIONS

1. The stayers are: Guffy, Wad, Showbuck, you, and Potzer. On the first round, you stayed with an open J and a pair of 5's in the hole. Each of you gets his fourth card. The open cards:

Guffy	A 2
Wad	10 K
Showbuck	Q 7
You	J 6
Potzer	9 4

Guffy checks. Wad bets. Showbuck calls. What do you do?

2. On the first round, your open K beat the board, and

you held a K 3 in the hole. You bet. Potzer, Mouse, and Brill called. Each of you gets his fourth card. The open cards:

Potzer	8 A
Mouse	Q A
Brill	7 J
You	K 4

Potzer bets. Mouse and Brill call. What do you do?

3. You stayed with a three-straight: a J open and a Q 10 in the hole. You catch a 7. There are three other stayers, none of whom shows much of anything. None of the cards you need for your straight shows, and you can get in for only two chips. Will you stay for at least one more card?

4. You stayed with a three-flush: the Club 7 open and the Club Q J in the hole. You catch the Diamond A. The open cards:

Brill	A Q
You	7 A
Pundit	3 J
Showbuck	10 5

You recapitulate: over the two rounds, the others have showed only two Clubs. Brill bets. Will you stay for one more card?

5. You stayed with a three-straight: the Spade Q open and the Heart J 10 in the hole. Now you catch the Heart 4; you have not improved your three-straight, but you have cought a three-flush. With three more cards available, will you stay for at least one?

6. The stayers are: Potzer, Pundit, Showbuck, Brill, and
you. The action has been heavy; there have been some trap
checks, but nobody indicates authentic weakness. The sixth
card is dealt. The open cards:

Pundit	J 5 J J
Showbuck	3 3 5 A
Brill	7 7 6 6
You	9 J K 2
Potzer	A 2 3 4

"The quality of mercy is not strained," Pundit says. "I
check."

"But my patience *is* strained," Showbuck says. "No
mercy." He tosses four chips into the pot.

"We'll see if there's any justice." Brill raises.

You have a pair of K's in the hole. Do you raise, call,
or fold?

7. The stayers are: Wad, Mouse, and you. The open
cards:

Wad	A 3 3 3
Mouse	5 5 4 4
You	Q J Q J

Wad, who has been winning, pushes four chips into the
pot. Mouse closes his eyes, better to review the previous
action. He remembers, as you do, that a 3 and two A's were
folded. He raises, and Wad winces.

You remember, in addition, that a 5 and a 4 were folded.
You show two pairs, Q's and J's; you hold a pair of K's in
the hole. All your cards are live. There are about fifty chips
in the pot, and you can get in for eight. Certainly, Wad will
not reraise. Do you call or fold?

8. The stayers are: Potzer, Mouse, and you. The seventh card is dealt in the hole. The open cards:

Potzer .... J 9 8 7
Mouse .... A J 4 A
You .... 3 3 2 J

Mouse bets. Your first two hole cards were K's, and you have just caught a 3 — a full house. Do you raise, call, or fold?

9. The only stayers are Brill and you. He shows a four-flush K 10 7 2. You show 10 9 8 7 in different suits, and you hold J J 3 in the hole. Brill checks. Do you bet your straight, or do you check?

10. The stayers are: you, Guffy and Showbuck. The seventh card is dealt in the hole. The open cards:

You .... A 10 9 7 of Hearts
Guffy .... Q 8 6 4
Pundit 6 5 4 2

You have just caught the Heart 3; you hold a flush. Your two other hole cards are 9's. You bet.

"I've counted Hearts all over the joint," Guffy says, "and I don't believe you." He feigns deep study of Pundit's open cards. "I don't believe you either. That's no straight. I'll tell you what I'm gonna do. I'm gonna . . ."

"Never mind the speech. Just do it," Pundit says.

"Very well." Guffy raises.

Pundit folds. "It's the possible flush over there I'm worried about, not you and your bushwah."

"I hate to lose you," Guffy says. "Now, let's see if he's worried about me."

Are you? Do you raise, call, or fold?

The Subsequent Action
ANSWERS

1. Guffy may be trying to conceal something, or he may fear Wad's possible bobtail. Showbuck sometimes makes irrational bets, but he probably holds a pair. You must contend with Potzer, too. Your hand is unpromising. Fold.

2. You are probably out in front, but you may not stay there. Raise; try to drive somebody out. You will confuse the issue in the process. The opposition will not necessarily read you for K's.

3. Fold. The odds against your catching the straight have lengthened to approximately 10 to 1.

4. Fold. The odds against your catching the flush have lengthened to approximately 11 to 1.

5. Yes, stay — call, but do not raise — unless you are confronted with raises, in which event you should fold.

6. Showbuck holds a full house, and Brill thinks his is higher. Potzer sees only his straight, or possible straight, and will stay. Pundit is unpredictable, but you know Showbuck will reraise, making it far too expensive for you to chase. Fold, even though the cards you need are live.

7. Any one of six cards will give you a lock. The money odds more than balance the odds against your catching your full house, so call.

8. Mouse, the epitome of caution, is betting into Potzer's possible straight. There can be only one reason: Mouse holds a big hand, a full house, and it is higher than yours. Fold.

9. Check along. Brill may be sandbagging. Why bet and give him the chance to raise?

10. Guffy's performance poses questions: While he might try to bluff you and Pundit individually, would he try to

bluff you collectively? Has he reasoned that the very au-
dacity of a bluff in the face of what are probably big hands
may enable him to get away with it? Showing trash, what
can he hold? A concealed full house? Is his chatter, as usual,
an indication of insecurity? Or has he, after a moment of
self-scrutiny, decided to use the chatter as a prop? Is he
overdoing it to get a raise, or at least a call, out of you?

The evidence is inconclusive. Regardless of the direction
in which you lean, I am sure a reasonable doubt remains.
It is a case in which you must buy the truth with a call.

High-Low

Through the decades, Sarge has seldom bypassed an opportunity to play Poker. The telephone rings, and he is invited to sit in with a new group.

"You may have found yourself a customer," he says. "What style of game?"

"Dealer's choice. A little of everything. High-Low and . . ."

"High-Low lets me out, thank you." Sarge's voice approaches absolute zero. "I play *real* Poker, not the crazy, hybrid games."

"If you gave High-Low a chance, you might enjoy it."

"I've given it plenty of chances. The trouble is it never gives *me* a chance. I never know who's doing what, and I don't care for the idea of dividing pots."

Sarge is typical of many old-timers who are eluded by the growing popularity of High-Low. They have only one valid argument: taste. They argue that High-Low is a hybrid game, but Poker in any form is a hybrid game. Early in the nineteenth century, French-speaking people of New Orleans bred their game of *poque* to *as nas*, a Persian import, and the offspring became known as Poker. It also has the genes of games from many other countries.

And what's wrong with a good hybrid? The most delectable vegetables, the most beautiful flowers, some marvelous cattle and dogs are all products of logical and careful hybridization. High-Low Poker is a scientific and exciting hybrid.

Another complaint is that it is not real Poker. High-Low is an eclectic extension of a basic Poker principle: ranking hands according to their scarcity. Some figures in evidence: The natural triplets, straights, flushes, full houses, four-of-a-kinds, and straight flushes total 74,628. The hands of comparable scarcity at the other end of the scale—the three lowest categories of hands below one pair — are the 8-highs, 7-highs, and 6-highs. Those runts total only 53,040.

For those who want a more complex, more difficult, more exhilarating form of Poker than the classical one-winner variations, High-Low is the answer.

At High-Low, the usual practice is to permit optional use of the A's: above the K's, or below the 2's. The lowest possible hand is 6 4 3 2 A, not in the same suit. Held in the same suit, those cards constitute a flush. Note that 5 4 3 2 A is a straight.

Low hands are ranked from the top down; 7 5 4 3 2 is lower than 7 6 3 2 A.

After the last round of betting, either of two ways may be used to declare for high or low: vocally or by means of chips.

Where the vocal method is used, the last raiser declares first; then the other stayers follow in clockwise order.

Where the chip method is used, each stayer, concealing his intent, reaches among his chips; all the stayers simultaneously extend and open their fists. One chip is a declaration for high. An empty fist is a declaration for low. The holder of the highest hand declaring for high and the holder of the lowest hand declaring for low divide the pot.

It is permissible to declare for *both* high and low, vocally or by means of two chips, according to group procedure. A stayer declaring for both must win both outright. If he is beaten or tied either way, he loses everything. The remaining stayers divide the pot, according to their declarations and hands.

To avert endless whipsawing, the number of raises during each round of betting must be limited.

8

Seven-Card High-Low Stud

The First Round

QUESTIONS

Dealt the same way as one-winner Seven-Card Stud, this is a variation favored among High-Low enthusiasts. The stakes in this group are one chip ante by each player; two chip limit, until a pair shows or the sixth card is dealt; then the limit is increased to four chips. Two raises per player per round are permitted. Stiff! The chip declaration is used. Sharp!

1. Potzer deals. The open cards:

Guffy	J
Wad	A
Pundit	8
Mouse	K

Showbuck 6
Brill 9
You .... A
Potzer 10

Wad bets. Pundit calls. Mouse folds. Showbuck raises. Brill folds. You have a pair of Q's in the hole. Do you raise, call, or fold?

2. Guffy deals. The open cards:

Wad 2
Pundit .... A
Mouse 4
Showbuck .... J
Brill 5
You .... K
Potzer 7
Guffy .... Q

Pundit bets. Mouse raises. Showbuck folds. Brill raises. You have an A K in the hole. Do you raise, call, or fold?

3. Wad deals. The open cards:

Pundit .... A
Mouse 7
Showbuck .... K
Brill 2
You .... A
Potzer 3
Guffy 10
Wad .... Q

Pundit bets. Mouse calls. Showbuck folds. Brill raises. You have A 3 in the hole. Do you raise, call, or fold?

4. Pundit deals. The open cards:

Mouse	J
Showbuck	A
Brill	3
You	Q of Clubs
Potzer	4
Guffy	6
Wad	9
Pundit	5

Showbuck bets. Brill calls. You have the J 10 of Clubs in the hole, a three-straight-flush, and only one Club shows elsewhere. Do you raise, call, or fold?

5. Mouse deals. The open cards:

Showbuck	5
Brill	A
You	10
Potzer	J
Guffy	7
Wad	7
Pundit	4
Mouse	9

Brill bets. You have A 2 in the hole. Do you raise, call, or fold?

6. Showbuck deals. The open cards:

Brill	3
You	8
Potzer	K
Guffy	3
Wad	6
Pundit	7

Mouse 2
Showbuck . . . . K

Potzer checks. Guffy bets. Wad calls. Pundit raises. Mouse calls. Showbuck folds. Brill raises. You have a pair of 8's in the hole. Do you raise or call?

7. Brill deals. The open cards:

You 7
Potzer 4
Guffy . . . . 9 ·
Wad . . . . A
Pundit 7
Mouse 5
Showbuck . . . . J
Brill . . . . Q

Wad bets. Pundit calls. Mouse raises. Showbuck calls. Brill folds. You have an 8 6 in the hole. Do you raise, call, or fold?

8. You deal. The open cards:

Potzer 8
Guffy 10
Wad 2
Pundit . . . . K
Mouse 6
Showbuck 3
Brill 10
You 4

Pundit checks. Mouse bets. Showbuck raises. Brill folds. You have a 4 2 in the hole. Do you raise, call, or fold?

9. Potzer deals. The open cards:

Guffy . . . . A

Wad 8
Pundit 2
Mouse 4
Showbuck 7
Brill .... J
You 8
Potzer 6

Guffy bets. Wad calls. Pundit raises. Mouse calls. Showbuck raises. Brill folds. You have 7 5 in the hole. Do you raise, call, or fold?

10. Guffy deals. The open cards:

Wad 9
Pundit 7
Mouse 2
Showbuck 3
Brill 6
You .... 4 of Diamonds
Potzer .... A
Guffy .... J

Potzer bets. Guffy folds. Wad calls. Pundit raises. Mouse calls. Showbuck raises. Brill calls. You have the Diamond A 2 in the hole. Do you raise, call, or fold?

The First Round

ANSWERS

1. If this were the high-hand-wins form of Seven-Card Stud, you would be happy with your pair of Q's. Here, you must fold because, as in most High-Low variations, the odds are in favor of the low hands. A hand which starts out

as a low may develop into a contending high; 5 4 3 may become a winning low or a straight. With your pair of Q's, you are virtually out of the running for low, and if you catch another pair you will be hooked. If you catch a winning high, you will get only half of the pot. Retire from the action now.

It is also unsound, in this variation, to stay with a pair of J's, 10's, 9's, or 8's.

2. Fold, because the price of staying with your pair of K's has become too high. When you can get in at a low price, a pair of K's constitutes a borderline call and requires delicate management thereafter.

3. Raise to cloud the issue; try to make the opposition read you for a promising low. Bear in mind that two pairs, A's-up, will show a profit over a series of sessions.

4. Fold. Do not stay with three-straight-flushes higher than 9 8 7. Do not stay with three-flushes higher than 9 7. Do not stay with three-straights higher than 8 7 6.

5. Fold. This is the type of hand which traps those who ignore the odds. The A 2 look promising, but the 10 fouls your hand. You want to catch a strong low, and that means a hand topped by the 8 or a lower card. You need three low cards out of the remaining four available to you, and you probably won't catch them. Recommended minimum staying requirement when you aim for low: 8-high in your first three cards.

6. Raise, and continue to raise at every opportunity, unless at some stage you are beaten in sight or otherwise convinced you are beaten. Your triplet 8's are a probable winner and with four more cards available, the odds are short against your catching a full house. Build the pot.

7. Raise. Your hand can develop either way. With a good catch, you may even win both ends.

8. Call. The 4's are live, and you may catch triplets. A low card will put you in the running the other way. But be careful if you pair your 2.

9. Ordinarily, you would stay with an 8 7 5, but in this deal the action indicates that you are running third or fourth for low, and I hope you are not thinking of catching a 7 and then trying to catch a straight. Fold, even though you do not believe everybody at the table.

10. Bang away — raise. You are off to a flying start. Your hand can develop into a lock for low, or into a flush, or even into a straight. If anybody raises after you, take your second raise. Plan to look at no less than two more cards.

The Subsequent Action
QUESTIONS

1. You stayed with an A open and an A 3 in the hole. The fourth card is dealt, and these show:

You	A 3
Potzer	7 9
Wad	2 8
Brill	6 4

Do you bet or check?

2. You stayed with a 6 open and a 6 4 in the hole. The fourth card is dealt, and these show:

Showbuck	7 A
You	6 4
Potzer	3 2
Guffy	5 9
Pundit	K Q

Showbuck bets. Do you raise, call, or fold?

3. You stayed with the Spade 7 open and the Spade 5 2 in the hole. The fourth card is dealt, and these show:

Brill	....	A 6
You	....	7 K of Spades
Pundit	....	4 A
Mouse	....	5 8
Showbuck	....	2 9

Brill bets. With your four-flush, do you raise, call, or fold?

4. You stayed with a 4 open and an 8 3 in the hole. The fourth card is dealt, and these show:

Potzer	....	A 8
Guffy	....	7 3
Wad	....	6 5
Showbuck	....	2 A
Brill	....	4 8
You	....	4 Q

Potzer checks. Guffy bets. Wad raises. Showbuck raises. Brill calls. Do you call or fold?

5. You stayed with a 2 open and a 6 5 in the hole. The fourth card is dealt, and these show:

Brill	....	5 5
You	....	2 7
Potzer	....	J 9
Guffy	....	A 8
Pundit	....	8 6

Brill bets. Do you raise, call, or fold?

6. Guffy, Mouse, and Brill showed picture cards on the first round and folded. The rest have stayed with you through the fifth card, and a big pot has been built — there have been raises and reraises galore on each round. The open cards:

Showbuck	10 Q Q
You	3 6 2
Potzer	3 4 9
Wad	4 6 7
Pundit	2 7 8

Showbuck bets four chips. You have an A 4 in the hole, a lock for low. Do you raise or call?

7. You stayed with three low cards. Your fourth card did not help, but you stayed through some heavy betting. The fifth card is dealt, and these show:

Wad	A 7 7
Pundit	5 8 J
Showbuck	4 7 A
Brill	6 A K
You	3 Q 6

Wad bets. Pundit calls. Showbuck raises. Brill calls. You have an A 6 in the hole; your 6 has just been paired. Do you call or fold?

8. There are only three staying with you through the fifth card. All their open cards are low, and they have been betting vigorously. The open cards:

Brill	8 2 A
You	7 3 5
Potzer	8 6 2
Guffy	4 6 K

Brill bets. You have a 5 3 in the hole. Do you raise, call, or fold?

9. Wad and Showbuck are the only ones still staying with you as the sixth card is dealt. The open cards:

> Showbuck .... J 4 J 4
> Wad .... A 8 4 2 of Hearts
> You .... 5 5 7 A

Showbuck gaily tosses in four chips, grins at you, and says, "You're in the middle, and I feel sorry for you, but Wad with his flush and low is going to have the real problem."

"You'll soon see who's got problems," Wad grunts.

Meanwhile, you are comfortable with a pair of A's in the hole and the memory of a folded J; Showbuck cannot have four of them. Do you raise or call?

10. Guffy, Mouse, Showbuck, and Brill have stayed with you, and all of them have raised frequently. As the seventh card is dealt, these show:

> Guffy .... 6 2 J 6
> Mouse 4 5 9 8
> Showbuck 7 3 8 5
> Brill 3 7 9 6
> You .... 5 2 Q 7

You have an A 3 in the hole. Your 7 5 3 2 A looks like a lock for low. You also hold an A-high flush.

Guffy examines his last hole card and says, "This is purely academic. I didn't need help." He bets four chips.

Mouse calls. Showbuck raises. Brill raises. Of course, you raise.

"Thank you for the cooperation, gentlemen," Guffy says. "My first raise. I've got another coming."

Mouse folds. Along with Guffy, Showbuck, Brill and you take all the permissible raises.

The pot is a whopper. Are you satisfied with half of it, or do you declare for both high *and* low?

The Subsequent Action

ANSWERS

1. Bet. You will get three chances to catch your full house. Even if you fail to improve, your A's-up may win the high half. Also, there is a remote chance of catching a winning low.

2. Fold. Unless you improve, you will be slaughtered. If you win the high half, it will be just that — half, and many of the chips will have come from your stack.

3. Call: do not reveal the strength of your hand, which can develop in either direction, or both.

4. Fold. Your chance of catching a strong high is too slim. You need two good catches for a strong low, two out of three, and even then it probably won't be strong enough.

5. Raise. You have the best prospects for the low half, so build the pot.

6. Call: that is the best way to lure more chips into the pot. If you raise, you may frighten some of your clients.

7. Fold. You need two good catches out of two for a strong low. The odds against your getting them are prohibitive.

8. Call. You have two chances to catch a full house. The

chance to catch a strong low, although remote, is also a factor.

9. Showbuck is probably faking, trying to steal the high half. He may have the case J in the hole, but even so, your full house beats his. The point is that Wad cannot know this, and he may have already decided to declare for both high and low. Don't discourage Wad. Call, without histrionics, unless you are an accomplished actor.

Wad will surely raise. Showbuck will reraise. Let them whipsaw you. Do not raise at any stage. When you get your seventh card, look at it without change of expression. Give Wad no inkling of the fact that this party is yours.

10. Guffy does not hold the full house. Mouse holds a mediocre low, perhaps a straight. Ditto for Showbuck. Brill holds a strong low, but it is not so strong as yours; for a change, he has misread the situation. Put two chips in your hand — go for both high and low. With a flush and a 7-high, it usually pays to do that. With a straight and a 7-high, it depends upon the open cards and your diagnosis of the mallarkey at the table.

9

Big Squeeze

"Six-Card Option" is another name for this testing varia-tion, which places premiums on memory, precise calcula-tion, and applied psychology. Big Squeeze is Six-Card High-Low Stud with a one-card draw at the end, and is dealt as follows: One card in the hole and one open, fol-lowed by the first round of betting. To each stayer, three more open cards are available, one at a time, and each is followed by a round of betting. The sixth card is dealt in the hole and is followed by a round of betting. Now comes the one-card draw, replacing the discard, in the hole or open, at the stayer's option, and it is followed by the final round of betting. A stayer may, of course, stand pat, for the purpose of deception or so as not to disturb a hand which may win both high and low.

Big Squeeze is closely related to Seven-Card High-Low Stud. In Big Squeeze, there is one more round of betting: the pots are bigger. The two variations present similar problems in the middle stages, which were covered in the preceding section, but the draw at the end of Big Squeeze is another matter: it often compels the stayer to make a difficult choice.

The stakes at Big Squeeze in this group are one chip ante by each player; two chip limit until a pair shows or the sixth card is dealt; then the limit is increased to four chips. Two raises per player per round are permitted. The chip declaration is used.

1. You have an open K which beats the board, and another K in the hole. Do you plan to stay?

2. Brill deals. The open cards:

You	7
Potzer	9
Guffy	A
Wad	Q
Pundit	8
Mouse	3
Showbuck	J
Brill	4

Guffy bets. Wad folds. Pundit and Mouse call. Showbuck raises. Brill folds. You have another 7 in the hole. Raise, call, or fold?

3. You deal. The open cards:

Potzer	2
Guffy	8
Wad	K

Pundit .... A
Mouse 10
Showbuck 6
Brill .... J
You .... A of Spades

Pundit bets. Mouse folds. Showbuck calls. Brill folds. You have the Spade 9 in the hole. Raise, call, or fold?

4. Potzer deals. The open cards:

Guffy .... Q
Wad 8
Pundit 5
Mouse 2
Showbuck 9
Brill 7
You 7
Potzer ...... J

Guffy checks. Wad bets. Pundit calls. Mouse and Showbuck fold. Brill calls. You have an 8 in the hole. Raise, call, or fold?

5. Guffy deals. The open cards:

Wad 4
Pundit ...... K
Mouse 2
Showbuck .... Q
Brill 5
You .... A
Potzer 10
Guffy .... A

You have a 6 in the hole and you bet. Potzer calls. Guffy raises. Wad calls. Pundit folds. Mouse calls. Showbuck folds. Brill raises. Do you raise, call, or fold?

6. In this and the remaining deals in this section, the sixth card has been dealt and the betting after the sixth card has been completed. Each stayer has four cards open and two cards in the hole. Now comes the draw. Brill is dealing, and you are under the gun. The open cards:

You	2 7 5 A
Potzer	4 9 3 7
Wad	6 3 A Q
Brill	5 6 4 3

You have a pair of 2's in the hole. Potzer and Brill can go either way: they have possible straights along with possible lows. You remember that a 7 and a 5 were folded early in this deal. How do you draw?

7. You started with a promising low hand and, although it has not lost all of its promise in that direction, it has turned into triplets. Ordinarily, you would be happy with them, but look at the open cards:

Showbuck	7 2 7 7
Brill	4 8 A 4
You	6 3 4 6
Potzer	Q 9 J 8
Pundit	3 8 7 A

Showbuck has been raising throughout. Pundit raised often early in this deal, but has taken to calling. Brill took all of his raises during the last round.

If Showbuck is aware of Potzer's possible straight, there is no reason to believe Showbuck is disturbed by it or that Potzer is aware of it, for that matter. Potzer is, in fact, somewhat groggier than usual.

"Right in the breadbasket," Showbuck says, as he discards from the hole.

Brill breaks his 4's and catches a 10. You have a 6 2

in the hole. How do you draw?

8. Continuing to bull the game, Showbuck has taken all his raises in this deal, too. Pundit and Mouse have hammered away. Nobody seems to fear you. The open cards:

```
You ..........   7 3 6 6
Pundit .......   4 5 8 Q
Mouse .......   A 2 8 9
Showbuck ....   4 2 J A
```

You have an A J in the hole. How do you draw?

9. You started with four low cards, then caught two pictures, but are still in there, hoping to catch the winning low in the draw. The open cards:

```
You ..........   3 7 2 K
Potzer ........   4 5 9 8
Guffy ........   7 3 6 Q
Pundit .......   8 7 K 5
```

You have an A Q in the hole. How do you discard?

10. You have caught a full house. The open cards:

```
Potzer ........   K 2 8 J of Diamonds
Wad .........   2 7 2 2
Showbuck ....   Q J 9 8
You ..........   3 2 5 5
```

Potzer discards from the hole and registers joy. Wad discards the 7 and catches a J. Showbuck, whose open cards are in different suits, stands pat.

"I'm telling you guys right now that nobody runs me out," he says.

"Why should anybody want to run you out?" Wad asks,

with a suspicious glance at your hand. You hold a 5 3 in the hole. What do you do?

ANSWERS

The staying requirements for this variation apply also to Six-Card High Low Stud without the draw at the end.

1. Stay, but be cautious. With no K's open elsewhere, wired K's warrant staying. To avoid advertising them, I suggest that you check; then, when the pot is opened, call. This procedure will also hold down the cost of your staying. Do not stay with wired Q's, J's, 10's, 9's, or 8's.

2. Call. Stay with wired 7's if none shows elsewhere. Stay in the same circumstances with wired 6's, 5's, 4's, 3's, or 2's. Stay with wired A's if no more than one shows elsewhere.

3. Fold, despite your A. Your 9 is too high.

4. Fold. Stay with 8 6 or lower two cards. Bet any two cards topped by a 7 or lower card vigorously.

5. Raise. Your prospects are excellent. Your hand is a shade better than Brill's for low: yours can become an immortal.

6. You can beat what you can see for high, but Brill's low is more promising than yours; he may already hold a lock. Go for the full house, although the odds are long against your catching it. Discard your 7 or 5, and hope for the best. Even if you fail to improve, you have a fair chance of winning with your triplet 2's.

7. Don't chase Showbuck's triplet 7's; discard your 6 from the hole and hope for a useful low catch. Also, you

may fill your inside straight: not a happy chance by itself, but of some value as an extra at no added charge.

8. Discard your J. If you split your 6's, and catch a high or pairing card, your J-high will probably be out of the contention for low. Give yourself the chance to improve significantly in either direction, the chance to catch triplet 6's or a strong low.

9. Discard your Q from the hole. You must improve to have a shot at low, and you may as well have your draw down.

10. Your open cards suggest that you hold a lock for low, so do not disturb them. Stand pat: you need no improvement. Then, all the other stayers will probably declare for high, giving you the whole pot.

If the vocal declaration were used, the situation would not be nearly so favorable to you, because you could be maneuvered into declaring before some of the others. Then, the last stayer to declare would simply beep, "Low" and get half of the pot, for no good reason.

The chip declaration makes a much sharper game, and I am all for it. The vocal declaration is for bisexual Poker.

10

Five-Card
High-Low Stud

Five-Card High-Low Stud is called "Sudden Death" because a promising low hand may pair up on the fourth or fifth card, and there is no payoff for finishing in the middle. It is dealt like the high-hand-wins variation and is a relatively mild game, unless played for high stakes. It moves quickly. The stakes in this group are one chip ante by each player; two chip limit until a pair shows or the fourth card is dealt; then the limit is increased to four chips. Two raises per player per round are permitted, and the chip declaration is used.

1. Brill deals. The open cards:

> You 10
> Potzer .... K

Guffy 7
Wad 2
Pundit .... Q
Mouse 8
Showbuck 5
Brill .... K

Potzer bets. Guffy and Wad call. Pundit raises. Mouse
folds. Showbuck calls. Brill folds. You have a 10 in the
hole. Raise, call, or fold?

2. You deal. The open cards:

Potzer .... K
Guffy 8
Wad 10
Pundit 8
Mouse 4
Showbuck .... J
Brill 7
You 9

Potzer bets. Guffy calls. Wad and Pundit fold. Mouse
calls. Showbuck raises. Brill calls. You have an A in the hole.
Raise, call, or fold?

3. Potzer deals. The open cards:

Guffy 9
Wad 5
Pundit .... A
Mouse .... Q
Showbuck 3
Brill 7
You 9
Potzer .... K

Pundit bets. Mouse folds. Showbuck raises. Brill calls. You have a J in the hole. Raise, call, or fold?

4. Guffy deals. The open cards:

Wad	6
Pundit	Q
Mouse	7
Showbuck	Q
Brill	8
You	5
Potzer	9
Guffy	A

Guffy bets. Wad calls. Pundit calls. Showbuck and Brill call. You have a 5 in the hole. Raise, call, or fold?

5. Wad deals the third card to four stayers. The open cards:

You	4 2
Potzer	Q K
Wad	J J
Showbuck	K 10

Wad bets. Showbuck folds. You have a 2 in the hole. Raise, call, or fold?

6. You deal the third card to your stayers, including yourself. The open cards:

Mouse	7 7
Showbuck	9 5
You	8 K
Guffy	8 A

Mouse checks. Showbuck bets. You have a 3 in the hole. Raise, call, or fold?

7. Potzer deals the fourth card to four stayers. The open cards:

> Guffy .... 2 Q 9
>
> Pundit .... 5 8 J
>
> Showbuck .... 6 J 8
>
> You 6 3 9

Guffy bets. The others call. You have a 2 in the hole. Raise or call?

8. Guffy deals the fourth card to three stayers. The open cards:

> Brill .... K 4 Q
>
> You 7 4 4
>
> Mouse .... J J 5

Mouse bets. Brill raises. You have the case 4 in the hole and you remember that a J was folded. Do you now raise or call?

9. Wads deals the fifth card to three stayers. The open cards:

> Pundit .... K 4 K Q
>
> Showbuck .... 3 K 5 K
>
> You .... 6 7 2 A

Pundit bets. Showbuck raises. You have an A in the hole. Raise or call?

10. Pundit deals the fifth card to four players. The open cards:

> Wad .... Q Q J 10
>
> Showbuck .... K 7 K A
>
> You 5 4 3 2
>
> Potzer 8 2 2 6

During the first two rounds, Wad raised at every opportunity. When Showbuck caught his second open King, he and you did the raising — you have an A in the hole. Potzer, who is adept at finding reasons for staying, has called throughout.

Now, Showbuck, after brief scrutiny of your open cards, stacks four chips. Wad tried to deter him: "Possible straight there."

"I'll see if he's really got it." Showbuck bets the four chips.

You raise, of course. Potzer, hoping your 5, 4, or 3 is paired, calls.

"I really should raise," he says, without giving his reason, such as it is.

"Jerks." Wad, who has a Q in the hole, calls.

Showbuck teases Wad by stacking eight chips. Wad mutters something. Showbuck grins and calls.

How do you declare?

ANSWERS

1. Call, and plan to stay all the way, unless beaten in sight or otherwise convinced you are beaten for high.

Five-Card High-Low Stud is unique among high-low variations in that the odds favor going for high, if possible, rather than for low. A high hand cannot worsen, whereas a low hand can.

2. Call. You have good prospects both ways: you may pair your A or catch low cards.

3. Fold. The J 9 combination is garbage in every variation I have ever seen except Baseball, where the 9's are wild.

4. Fold. Potzer will surely stay — he always does — and Guffy, with his open A, probably will. Against so many stayers, your 5's are too weak for high; the odds are against your improving. And you would be giving too much of an advantage to those aiming for low.

5. Raise: try to drive Guffy out. You may be able to steal the low half and, if you catch another 2 or pair your 4, you will probably win the high half. The way things are going, you could win the whole pot by improving for high. It is unlikely that your raise will be interpreted as indicating a pair.

6. Fold. It is bad enough to chase in one direction; it is worse to chase in two.

7. Raise. You are far out in front of the opposition for low; with only one more card to be dealt, the odds are in your favor, so make the chasers pay. The fifth card may foul up your hand, but it is more likely to give you a lock for low.

8. Call. A raise would reveal the nature of your hand. Brill probably holds a pair of K's, and you want him to declare for high so you can take the whole pot.

9. Pundit holds a second pair, or an A in the hole, and is committed to high. Showbuck certainly holds a second pair and refuses to credit Pundit with one. You hold a lock for low: your A's count as 1's. Raise and declare for low.

10. Put two chips in your hand: declare for both high and low. Your straight is a lock for high. You have the right, also, to rank your A above the K, making your hand an A-high runt, as well as a straight. Take it all.

11

Break for a Snack

"Let's separate the men from the boys," Pundit says, as he gives the deck a loud riffle. "What I'm gonna deal is . . ."

"Before you start dealing it," Wad cuts in, "let's take a break for a snack."

The winners get up more or less willingly, the losers reluctantly. At the buffet, the winners eat more, per capita, than the losers. All the men, except Showbuck and Pundit, drink coffee. Showbuck wins some attention by mixing a martini, extra dry, for himself. Pundit asks for milk: he has an ulcer.

Pundit owns a jobbing business which he is continually expanding. The driving force behind his enterprise is his wife, Polly. She is also the driving force behind the ulcer.

Polly is a platinum blonde who needs falsies, and a heavy girdle to bale her ponderous buttocks; she has the voice of command. Naturally, Polly would not permit herself to be alone on Pundit's Poker night. She has invited the wives to her home for cards. Present are:

Doris Wad, dark, short, small-boned, and shrill —

Terry Showbuck, henna-haired and buxom —

Caroline Mouse, silver-tipped and trim — she plays cards with cheerful earnestness —

Mabel Guffy, hazel-eyed and gentle — she is the group patsy at whatever game is in vogue. Brill's wife, Gloria, and Sue Potzer were also invited; they are attending a meeting of the Women's Civic Improvement Association. They may drop in later.

After a three-year defection to Samba, via Canasta, the game of choice is again Bridge. Mabel Guffy has cut out of this rubber and turned on the TV: a detergent epic. The players pay more attention to the TV than to the cards. Morality triumphs, and as the volume of canned applause increases, Polly bounces to the switch and wins the race with the commercial.

"Now we can concentrate on Bridge," Caroline says.

"Just a minute." Polly dashes out to the dining room. She returns in a gold-and-black kimono. "Everything is piping hot. Let's eat, girls. Something I whipped together in a jiffy."

Polly has whipped together egg rolls, barbecued spareribs, eggs foo yung, chicken chow mein, fried rice, boiled rice, soy sauce, sweet-and-sour sauce, hot mustard, almond cookies, fortune cookies, kumquats and tea.

"Oh, how lovely!" Caroline says.

"You must have read my mind," Terry says. "I've been dying for some Chinese food."

Mabel grabs a sparerib and chews on it. "Yum-yum."

"Some spread." Doris looks archly at Polly's rump.

"Pundit doesn't complain." Polly stares contemptuously at Doris's rump. "Take a seat, dearie, and see if you can fill a quarter of it."

Terry laughs. Doris forces a giggle. Caroline and Mabel act as if they had not heard the sally.

The women sit down and eat, praising Polly's ingenuity — assure her of the superiority of her meal over anything they could get even at the famous Canton Corner. But they leave most of the food, for two reasons: (1) it has the laundry flavor characteristic of Chinese dishes prepared by American housewives, and (2) there was too much of it in the first place.

Surveying all that leftover food, Polly resolves to serve it to Pundit at dinner the next two nights, except for the sauces — a concession to his ulcer. Thinking of him, she thinks also of his Poker game.

"I wonder how late the men will play tonight," she says.

Caroline looks at her watch. "They're good for a couple more hours." She would like to resume the Bridge game.

The others have had enough Bridge for tonight. Terry says, "The worst trouble with our culture is the separation of the sexes. I don't mind the boys having their night by themselves — it's a healthy thing for them — but why can't we do things together like we used to?"

"That's what *I* often ask myself," Caroline says.

"Why don't we do something about it instead of just yakking?" Terry asks.

"So I'll yak out an idea." Doris snaps her fingers. "Listen. If you're not all busy a week from Saddy night, bring your men to my house. Dinner at six; then we'll all play Poker together — the men with the women."

Caroline gives her a hug. "Grand! Count Mouse and me in."

Mabel says she has a previous engagement for that night but, without hesitation, promises to break it and be present with Guffy.

The others also accept. Terry says, "I'm sure the men will enjoy it, even though they'll make jokes about it."

"I'll ask Gloria and Sue, too," Doris says. "And that other couple. The men have a new player tonight."

Polly makes a quick tally. "That'll be sixteen people — too many for Poker."

Doris is equal to the problem: "I'll have two tables. I won't let any husband-and-wife combination sit at the same table."

Mabel shakes her head. "It won't work. The men will pre-empt one table for their regular game, and we'll be stuck at the other."

"Leave that to me," Doris says. "I aim to have a little talk with Wad beforehand."

Polly nods. She will have a little talk beforehand with Pundit.

Mabel winces as she anticipates a cutting retort when she breaks the news to Guffy. Nevertheless, she is determined. So are Terry and Caroline. So will Gloria and Sue be.

Some of the men will learn tonight, and the others will learn tomorrow morning, that they have been sentenced to a session of bisexual Poker. Meanwhile, they go happily back to their game. The losers are in their seats ahead of the winners.

Wild Card Variations

Some of the wild card variations which the women will concoct at Doris's party will be about as appetizing to the men as a mixture of pickled herring and ice cream. The interpolation of such variations by inept players can foul up serious games, but this, too, is true: The many rational wild card variations are as logical as, and much more difficult than, the classical natural variations.

Wild card variations increase the skilled player's advantage. Did you know that adding the wild Joker to the deck — only one wildy! — makes triplets more numerous than two pairs? The entire structure of the game changes, but the principles remain the same. To facilitate comparisons, I have placed the odds tables for the natural and wild card variations in the same section of this book. See

Chapter 18, "The Structure of Poker."

Wild cards create an added category: the five of a kinds, from the A's down to the Deuces. They rank above the straight flushes, from the royal flushes down.

As Pundit is about to deal, Potzer gets an inspiration. He says to Guffy, "My luck hasn't been running too well, and neither has yours. How about changing seats with me?"

Guffy is obliging. He does not say what he is thinking: that Potzer would do better to change his tactics.

So now Guffy is immediately to your left, and Potzer to his left.

12

Spit in the Ocean

There are hundreds of forms of Spit in the Ocean — some closed, some open, some natural, some with wild cards. All are based on this idea: to each player is dealt a hand consisting of a predetermined number of cards — as few as three, as many as seven. In the center of the table, one or more cards are turned up. The card or cards in the center are community property: each player may, *in his mind*, and as he chooses, adapt one, or some, or all of them to his hand.

This group plays Spit in the Ocean in a time-tested way, as follows: Each player gets an original, closed, four-card hand. One card is turned up in the center; it is wild and, of course, every player uses it. In addition, every other card of the same rank in a player's hand is wild. For example:

An 8 is turned up. You hold A A 3 8. The 8 in your hand is wild, and you may use the open 8 in the center of the table to make four A's.

Anybody may open the betting, in proper order, on anything. After that round of betting, there is a draw. A player may draw as many as four cards, because there is no rule against being ridiculous. After the draw comes the final round of betting. The stakes are the same as in natural Jackpots.

Bear this in mind: while only four cards are wild by designation, every stayer uses the center card. In practice, therefore, there are as many wild cards as stayers, plus the other three of the same rank.

1. Pundit deals. Remember that Potzer and Guffy have exchanged seats, so you are under the lip. Your hand: 6 6 K Q.

Wild card in the center: 10.

The pot is opened — there is no raising — you can get in for only two chips. Do you?

2. Mouse deals. Your hand: A J 9 5, all Clubs.

Wild card in the center: 3.

Showbuck bets. Brill folds. Do you raise, call, or fold?

3. Showbuck deals. Your hand: K J 10 5, in different suits.

Wild card in the center: 5.

Brill bets. Do you raise or call?

4. Brill deals. Your hand: 4 4 4 K.

Wild card in the center: J.

Do you bet or check?

5. You deal. Your hand: Q Q 7 7.

Wild card in the center: 2.

Guffy checks. Potzer bets. Wad raises. Pundit and Mouse fold. Showbuck calls. Do you raise, call, or fold?

6. Guffy deals. Your hand: K K 10 A.
Wild card in the center: K.
Wad checks. Pundit bets. Mouse folds. Showbuck raises. Brill folds. Do you raise, call, or fold?

7. You stayed with: Spades J 10, Heart 8, and Club 6.
Wild card in the center: 6.
How do you draw?

8. You stayed, happily, with: J J J 2.
Wild card in the center: 4.
You discarded your 2, and caught a futile 5, but you still have your four J's.
Guffy, who drew two, bets. Pundit, who drew one, calls. Showbuck, who drew two, folds. Do you raise, call, or fold?

9. You stayed with: Heart 10 8 7, Diamond 5.
Wild card in the center: 5.
The other stayers are: Potzer, Wad and Pundit; each drew one. You, with your straight flush, stand pat, of course.
Potzer now opens the betting. Wad raises. Pundit folds. Do you raise, call, or fold?

10. You stayed, happily, with K K 10 3.
Wild card in the center: K.
Guffy opened the betting. The other stayers are: Showbuck, who called — and Brill, who raised. I presume you raised. The others called.
Guffy draws one. Showbuck draws two. Brill draws one. How do you draw?

ANSWERS

1. Fold. Lacking a wild card in your own hand, you are bucking prohibitive odds. There are twenty-eight closed cards in your opponents' hands. One or more of them almost certainly hold 10's. At least one of them probably holds a pair higher than yours.

2. Fold. A flush is trash in this variation.

3. Call, but not because you hold the straight, which is virtually worthless. Stay because the wild 5 in your own hand, plus the wild 5 in the center, give you triplet K's. Plan to draw two cards to your K 5, and hope to catch at least four K's.

4. Check, with a view to calling unless there is a great deal of raising. Lacking a J in your own hand, you must assume that there are J's in opposing hands. Your prospects for improvement are poor, and your four 4's are not very strong.

5. Fold. Do not play a full house in this variation. A full house means no wild cards in your own hand.

6. With two wildies in your own hand, your prospects are excellent. In this situation, your four A's are close to a lock. Call: keep the entry fee low for Guffy and Potzer.

7. Discard the Heart 8 and draw one. Either of the two remaining 6's — or the Spade A, K, Q, 9, 8, or 7 — will give you a straight flush. Any J or 10 will give you four of a kind.

8. Most probably, Guffy and Pundit hold four of a kinds. Your four J's look good. Raise.

9. It is difficult to determine whether you are first, second, or third in this pot. Call, remembering that in such situations a straight flush warrants only a modicum of optimism.

10. This deal presents some tricky probability problems.

You know Brill holds one of the outstanding wild K's and Guffy or Showbuck holds the other. On the basis of past performance, credit it to Guffy; Showbuck probably does not belong in this pot.

Guffy's opening bet, subsequent call, and one-card draw indicate a respectable four of a kind. He probably has not improved.

Showbuck has been fishing: omit him from your calculations.

Brill probably has a big four of a kind; his raise was an effort to protect it. Credit him with four A's, or at least four Q's.

If you discard your 10 3 and draw two, the chances are you will not catch a card high enough to beat Brill's four of a kind. Try for five of a kind or a straight flush. If you draw two, the odds against catching five of a kind will be approximately 16 to 1. If you draw one, the odds against catching five of a kind will be 15 to 1. It is more probable that one of your opponents holds a 10 than a 3. So discard your 10 and draw one.

13

Jackpots with the Wild Joker

Reaching for the box in which the cards came, Showbuck says, "We'll go back to Draw — with a little modification." He extracts the Joker, which is new-clean, in contrast with the rest of the deck.

"That Joker will stick out like Jayne Mansfield," Guffy says.

"Yeah," Wad says, "It's about time we broke out a new pack." He provides it.

Being sure to include the Joker, Showbuck riffles eight times, cuts, riffles again.

"You don't have to wear the spots off them," Wad says.

Showbuck gives a final riffle. "Jackpots." He passes the deck to Mouse.

Mouse cuts. "How are you going to use the Joker?"

"If I'm lucky enough to catch it," Showbuck says, "I'm going to use it completely wild. You guys can use it any way you like."

"Good," Potzer says. "The Joker makes Jackpots a livelier game."

Potzer is wrong. Inclusion of the Joker produces more hands from triplets up, but actually induces greater conservatism in those who understand the structure of this fifty-three-card game.

1. Showbuck deals. Brill checks. You hold A A K 6 2. Bet or check?

2. Brill deals. You hold Joker J 7 4 2. Bet or check?

3. Wad deals. Mouse, Showbuck, and Brill check. You hold A A Q Q 4. Bet or check?

4. You deal. The others check around to you. You hold 10 10 5 5 A. Bet or check?

5. Mouse deals. Showbuck and Brill check. You hold 2 2 2 K 4. Bet or check?

6. Guffy deals. Potzer and the others check. You hold Q Q 9 9 7. Bet or check?

7. Mouse deals. Showbuck bets. Brill folds. You hold J 8 4 3 in different suits, and the Joker. Raise, call, or fold?

8. Along with you, the stayers are: Pundit, who opened the betting, and Brill. Pundit draws three. Brill draws two. You hold Spade 10 9, Heart 5 2, and the Joker. How do you draw?

9. Along with you, the stayers are: Potzer, who opened the betting, and Mouse. Potzer draws one. Mouse draws three. You hold 9 6 3 2 in different suits, and the Joker. You are permitted to draw as many as you want. How do you draw?

10. You stayed, along with Guffy and Mouse. Guffy drew two and Mouse drew one. You drew one to 10 9 8 7, and you caught a 6; you now hold a straight. Guffy bets. Mouse folds. Do you raise or call?

ANSWERS

1. Superficial consideration would make it seem that, with only one wild card added, the opening requirements are not greatly changed. Actually, Jackpots with the Wild Joker is a complicated variation, much trickier than many variations played with several wild cards.

The fact that there is only one wild card amplifies its importance. Estimating your chances before the draw is a two-phase operation based on this question: Is it probable that the Joker is in one of your opponents' hands?

Position becomes extremely important. That Brill has checked suggests he does not hold the Joker. There are six players after you, and they hold a total of thirty cards — more than half of the deck. It is probable that one of them holds the Joker. Therefore, you, lacking the Joker, should check with your pair of A's.

In a game with eight hands, when you are in a position where it is probable somebody due to act after you holds the Joker, do not open the betting with anything less than triplets.

The sixth seat is critical. If the sixth, seventh, or eighth seat, you may open with one pair of A's, or one pair of K's and a side A.

2. Bet. Holding the Joker, open in any position if it makes one pair of J's or better.

3. Check. You need triplets or better to open in this position, when you lack the Joker.

4. Fold. Do not stay with two short pairs in this variation under any circumstances.

5. Bet, but proceed with caution thereafter.

6. Bet. In the sixth position or later, two pairs, J's-up or better, warrant the risk. You probably won't get many stayers.

7. Call, with a view to holding the Joker-J and drawing three.

8. Keep the Spade 10 9 along with the Joker, and draw two. Any K Q, or K J, or Q J, or Q 8, or 8 7, or 8 6, or 7 6 will give you a straight. Any 10 or 9 will give you triplets. Any other pair will make triplets with your Joker. And there are some long shots: any two Spades will give you a flush; any 10 9 will give you a full house; any pair of 10's or 9's will give you four of a kind.

9. It is doubtful that you should have stayed. Being in there, do not make the mistake of drawing four: it is a 2 to 1 bet you will not catch a pair among them. Your best chance is to hold the Joker 9 and to draw three.

10. Raise. A natural straight is still a strong hand. Guffy probably drew two to triplets, or to the Joker with two related cards. He probably failed to improve. Of course, he may have caught a big hand and may reraise, but I think you should take that risk.

14

Low Hole Card Wild

If you have played this slam-bang variation of Seven-Card Stud, you know you usually need at least four of a kind to win the pot. The standard dealing procedure for Seven-Card Stud is followed in Low Hole Card Wild. Each player gets two cards in the hole and one card open, before the first round of betting. If a player stays all the way, and the temptations are many, he gets his seventh card in the hole.

The lowest hole card in a hand at the finish, and all open cards of the same rank in that hand, are wild *for that hand.*

The assassin in this variation may be that seventh card. For example: you have 4 3 in the hole and A A 3 3 open. Your 3's are wild at this stage, so you have five A's — a lock! — or is it? The seventh card, in the hole, is a 2. Now, your 2 is your only wild card, and your hand has become four 3's: very far from a lock. Revolting development.

The stakes in this group are one chip ante by each player; two chip limit until a pair shows or the last card is dealt; then the limit is increased to four chips.

1. You have 10 10 in the hole and 4 open. Stay or fold?

2. You have 3 Q in the hole and Q open. Stay or fold?

3. You have A A in the hole and 7 open. Stay or fold?

4. You have 2 7 in the hole and A open. Bet or check?

5. You have 2 2 in the hole and 3 open. Stay or fold?

6. Guffy deals. The open cards:

Potzer	8
Wad	J
Pundit	4
Mouse	2
Showbuck	K
Brill	10
You	K of Hearts
Guffy	5

Showbuck bets. Brill folds. You have a 2 and the Heart Q in the hole. None of the open cards elsewhere are Hearts within range of the royal flush you hope to catch. Raise, call, or fold?

7. Pundit deals. The open cards:

Mouse	A
Showbuck	Q

Brill	3
You	9
Guffy	6
Potzer	K
Wad	K
Pundit	4

Mouse bets. Showbuck folds. Brill calls. You have 9 9 in the hole. Raise, call, or fold?

8. There are four stayers and the fourth card is dealt. The open cards:

Guffy	A 7
Pundit	Q 8
Showbuck	8 K
You	J 3

Guffy bets. Pundit calls. Showbuck raises. You have J 3 in the hole. Raise, call, or fold?

9. The fifth card is dealt to four stayers. The open cards:

Potzer	4 A A
Wad	Q 3 Q
Brill	2 K K
You	8 8 J

Potzer bets. Wad folds. Brill calls. You have 4 8 in the hole. Raise, call, or fold?

10. The seventh card is dealt to three stayers. The open cards:

Guffy	A 3 4 7
Mouse	J J 2 4
You	Q 4 K K

Guffy checks. Mouse bets. Your first two hole cards were 4 Q. You have just caught a 3 in the hole; your four K's have become a full house. Call or fold?

1. Fold. Your last hole card will probably be lower than your 10's: there are more lower than higher cards outstanding. You do not figure to catch anything better than four 10's which is not much of a goal in this variation.

2. Stay with enthusiasm. The odds are long against your catching a last hole card below your 3. You know where you are going, and your prospects are bright.

3. The A's may be tempting, but you should fold. Your last hole card is almost certain to be lower than your A's. You will have no way of evaluating your prospects as you go along, unless you catch a third A. It is folly to stay when one cannot know what one is doing.

4. Check and, if anybody opens, fold. You must catch another A or 2 in a hurry to have a reasonable chance, and the odds are against you.

5. Stay and bet vigorously. You have two wild cards which will remain wild; your potential is tremendous, despite that open 3.

6. Fold. The royal flush alone is not worth hunting. The K and 2, which are open elsewhere, make your chance of improving in any other direction slim.

7. Raise now and raise at every opportunity, unless at some stage of the deal you are convinced you are beaten. You are sure of at least four of a kind, and you may do better. By raising, you will probably lose a few clients, but the stayers' added chips will compensate. Moreover, you will give yourself greater percentage.

8. Raise. You can beat what you can see, and your wild 3's will almost certainly stay wild, whereas your opponents' hands may be wrecked when that last card is dealt in the hole.

9. Fold. Brill would not stay with less than four K's in the face of Potzer's open cards. You are probably running second at best with your four 8's. Don't chase.

10. You are the victim of a card caprice, but you were right in staying to the seventh card. When your wild cards are 4's, 3's, or 2's, you have an excellent margin of safety, and this deal does not disprove the point. What to do now? Fold and save four chips. A full house is small stuff in this variation. We know Mouse, and we are sure he holds more.

15

Baseball

Scorned by purists and avoided by those whose tastes run to more peaceful games, this intricate form of Stud is the choice of dealers who want sparkling action and big pots. Baseball is Seven-Card Stud, explosively modified so:

The 9's are wild.

Any 3 dealt in the hole is wild, gratis. Any 3 dealt open imposes on its recipient this choice: he must consider himself struck out and must immediately fold — or if he elects to stay, he must match the pot, that is, put in as many chips as are already there. A bought 3 is, of course, wild. Usual practice is to put a ceiling on the price of a 3 and to increase the limit thereafter so that the buyer may protect his hand and the sandbagger may rejoice.

Any 4 dealt open entitles its holder to an additional hole

card, dealt to him immediately or at the end of that round, according to group prearrangement. It is not unusual for a player to catch a pair of open 4's and to finish with five hole cards.

The stakes in this group are one chip ante by each player; two chip limit thereafter until an open pair lacking the 3 is dealt; then the limit is increased to four chips. The ceiling on the price of an open 3 is twenty-five chips and, after a 3 has been bought, any stayer may bet as many as eight chips. If no open pair is dealt (a rarity), the limit is increased to four chips for the last round of betting.

1. No wild cards show. You have A open and A K in the hole. If you can stay for only two chips, will you do so?

2. No wild cards show. You have J open and J J in the hole; no J's show elsewhere. Do you plan to stay or fold?

3. You have K open and 9 8 in the hole. Do you plan to stay or fold?

4. You have 7 open and 7 3 in the hole. Do you plan to stay or fold?

5. You have Spade J and a 9 in the hole. Your first open card is the Spade 4, so you get another hole card: the Spade 7. Do you plan to stay or fold?

6. Brill deals. You are under the gun. You have Diamond K Q in the hole. Your first open card is a 3, which will cost you only eight chips, if you decide to buy it. Pundit says, "It'll never be cheaper." Do you buy or strike out?

7. You deal. The open cards:

Guffy .... J

Potzer 4
Wad .... 3 (he bought it)
Pundit .... K
Mouse 9
Showbuck 4
Brill 2
You .... A

Since Wad's 3 gives him a minimum of one pair, he opens the betting, with eight chips. Pundit folds. Mouse calls. Showbuck and Brill fold. You have A 9 in the hole. Raise, call, or fold?

8. Guffy deals. The open cards:

Potzer .... Q
Wad 10
Pundit 4
Mouse 8
Showbuck 6
Brill .... A
You 3

Before Guffy may deal himself his first open card, you must make your decision. You have 9 2 in the hole. Do you buy the 3?

9. Potzer deals. The open cards:

Wad .... A
Pundit 3
Mouse .... Struck out
Showbuck .... J
Brill 7
You 4
Guffy 8
Potzer 9

Pundit bets under the limit: four chips. "I'm giving everybody a bargain," he says. Showbuck says, "I can't resist it," and calls. Brill folds. You have 4 4 3 in the hole. Raise, call, or fold?

10. Showbuck deals. Brill buys a 3. Your first card is also a 3. You have J 9 in the hole. Do you buy?

The First Round

ANSWERS

1. Fold. Do not play a mere pair lacking a wild card.

2. Fold. Do not stay with natural triplets lower than Q's; this is a stiff but sound requirement.

3. Plan to stay, unless the price becomes too high.

4. Fold. Do not play a wild card with a pair lower than 8's.

5. Fold. It is futile to seek a mere flush or straight in Baseball. Usually, you need at least four of a kind to win.

6. Reject the 3. If the wild card were free, a 9, you would be justified in staying. Matching the pot with your hand is illogical.

7. Wad must have a wild card in the hole. Figure Mouse for a wild card in the hole, too. Although you have triplet A's, you have only one wild card. That leaves only five cards which can improve your A's — the two remaining A's and three wild cards. Fold; the odds against you are much too long. Wad and/or Mouse will probably move out in front of you before long.

8. Buy the 3, as in most instances where you have another wild card in the hole at this stage.

9. Pundit is being coy with some strong stuff in the hole, probably two hidden wild cards. Showbuck knows it; he is probably chasing with one wild card in the hole. Observe Potzer's open 9. You can count on him to come in. The money odds are satisfactory but, barring a miracle, five 4's are the best you can hope to catch, and they may not be good enough to win this pot. On the next round of betting, Pundit will raise the price. Be prudent: fold now.

10. Brill has one wild card in the hole, and may have two. Your hand may be as good as his, but you will have to pay sixteen chips for your 3, whereas Brill paid only eight. Why pay double the price for merchandise which may be inferior? Fold.

Baseball is also played High-Low, a wonderful blend of calculation, conjecture, and murder. The perfect low is 6 4 3 2 A; note that it must contain at least one wild card. The trap is the 5 held with other low cards: it may steer you into a 6-5-high, which is dangerous, because perfect lows are far from uncommon.

If you decide to play High-Low Baseball, I suggest these minimum staying requirements on the first round:

Two or more wild cards.

One wild card and any two different cards from among these — A 2 4 6.

One wild card and one pair of A's or K's.

Three natural A's.

The Subsequent Action

QUESTIONS

This group continues with the original form of Baseball

in which the high hand wins the whole pot.

1. The fourth card is dealt to four stayers. The open cards:

Guffy	3 J
Mouse	4 6
Brill	K K
You	A 3

You have A 9 in the hole. There are forty-six chips in the pot, and you must put in twenty-five if you decide to buy the 3. Do you?

2. The fourth card is dealt to four stayers. The open cards:

Potzer	Q 4
Wad	7 7
Pundit	J 5
You	A 3

You have K 9 in the hole; your A and K are in the same suit. There are fifteen chips in the pot. Do you match it?

3. The fourth card is dealt to five stayers. The open cards:

Guffy	10 9
Wad	A 4
Pundit	K 8
Showbuck	2 2
You	A 3

You have 9 7 in the hole. There are seventeen chips in the pot. Do you match it?

4. The fifth card is dealt to three stayers. The open cards:

```
Mouse   .......   4 9 3
Showbuck  ....   9 J 8
You  ..........   K 9 5
```

You have K 3 in the hole. On the second round, when you caught your four K's, you opened the betting, and Mouse raised. Showbuck and you then called.

Mouse has just built up the pot to fifty-three chips by buying the 3, and he bets eight. Showbuck folds. Do you call or fold?

5. The fifth card is dealt to four stayers. The open cards:

```
You  ..........   9 5 3
Potzer  ........   Q Q
Wad  .........   K 9
Brill  .........   A 4 of Clubs
```

You have 9 5 in the hole. There are thirty-six chips in the pot. Do you pay twenty-five for the 3?

6. The sixth card is dealt to three stayers. The open cards:

```
Pundit   .......   4 J 9 4
Showbuck  ....   9 Q Q 7
You  ..........   K A A 3
```

You have K 9 in the hole. There are forty chips in the pot. Do you pay twenty-five for the 3?

7. The sixth card is dealt to four stayers. The open cards:

```
Potzer  .......   K Q J 10 of Diamonds
Guffy  ........   7 7 9 7
Pundit  .......   8 8 5 A
You  ..........   3 J J 3
```

This is a huge pot, consisting largely of chips put in by you. You have 9 J in the hole; the 3 just dealt to you is superfluous. Do you buy it. There's another card to come — an opponent may improve.

8. The sixth card is dealt to four stayers. The open cards:

Guffy	5 K 9 5
Mouse	A 2 6 A
Brill	9 8 7 2
You	6 J 10 2

Mouse bets. Brill folds. You have 9 3 in the hole, but your open cards are in different suits: you have a straight and no chance of catching a straight flush. Do you call or fold?

9. The seventh card is dealt to three stayers. The open cards:

Potzer	A 9 2 A
Showbuck	7 A 5 5
You	6 6 K Q

Potzer bets. Showbuck folds. You have 3 9 10 in the hole, but your open K Q are in different suits, so the best you can make of your cards is four 6's. Do you raise, call, or fold?

10. The seventh card is dealt to four stayers. The open cards:

Wad	A 4 J 9
Mouse	9 K Q 3
Brill	J J 9 2
You	K 10 Q 8 of Spades

Mouse bets eight chips. Brill calls. You have 9 3 K in the hole: a royal flush. Raise, call, or fold?

The Subsequent Action

ANSWERS

1. Buy it. The 3 puts you well out in front, with four chances to catch an immortal. If anybody wants to chase you, all the better for you.

2. Match it. With a wild card in the hole, and an A Q, the risk is reasonable in view of what you can see.

3. Strike out. At this stage, you should not buy a 3, unless it gives you four of a kind or unless you have another wild card and two cards higher than the J.

4. It is not so close as it may seem. Mouse has shelled out for the 3, and he already has three hole cards. Read him for five of a kind, possibly two wild cards and an A in the hole. If you chase him, at eight chips a card, and if you catch five K's, you may still lose. Fold.

5. This one *is* close. The 3 will give you five 5's, putting you out in front, but with only two more cards to come, your chances of improving are poor. Read Wad for four K's. Potzer may have four Q's. Brill is out of the running, but Wad and Potzer will stay. The price is too high, and you should fold.

6. Pundit already has four cards in the hole: too much of a handicap for you to try to overcome. Fold. It is imprudent, as a rule, at this stage, to buy the 3 unless it creates a lock.

7. You have undoubtedly observed that, even if any one of your opponents were given three wild hole cards, your hand would remain a lock. Try to appear distraught as you buy the 3. Your histrionics may persuade somebody to stay with you all the way.

8. While a straight does, on occasion, win a Baseball pot, the holder is usually the group's principal contributor

over the long pull. Fold.

9. You have only one man to beat. Your hand is not very strong. Still, you do hold four 6's, and the price is only four chips, so call. For all you know, Potzer may be getting frisky with a mere full house, or three A's.

10. Mouse, who is aware of your possible royal flush, has bet into it. Brill has called. Surely, you credit Mouse with five K's or Q's and Brill with five J's. And don't forget Wad; he may yet display the winning hand. I think you should trust your judgment and fold.

16

About Players

No game is influenced more by personalities than is Poker; that is why I am including a quiz on probable behavior indicated by conversation. Imagine that you are meeting each of these gentlemen for the first time:

1. As Josh enters the room, you hear somebody say, "Everything that bird touches turns to gold. He knows how to invest his money."
What brand of Poker do you suppose Josh will play?

2. Chuck reports, "I hit the crap tables at Las Vegas for a couple of grand again — clipped the one-armed bandits, too."
Does this suggest anything about Chuck at the Poker table?

3. "Isn't it about time we raised the stakes?" somebody says. Mike refuses.

"With taxes so high, I don't feel like blowing a bundle here," he says.

"Aaa, you win enough from us."

"Maybe so," Mike says, "but our present limit is all I can afford."

How do you size him up?

4. The pregame conversation switches to baseball. Marty says, "Walter Johnson was the greatest southpaw pitcher who ever lived. Many a time, I saw ol' Walter strike out the side."

If you are not a baseball fan, you may miss the nuances here.

5. "Speaking of baseball," Doc says, "The Yankees play the Orioles Friday night — ought to be a terrific game. How about all of us going down together? My ticket broker always gets me wonderful seats. I'll phone him tomorrow. If he doesn't come through for me, I know somebody who will for sure. I usually have late office hours Friday, but I'll get away early this time. Who's with me?"

Does this oration tell you anything significant about Doc?

6. "Shake hands with Cal," your host says. "Watch out for this burglar. He's been taking us over for years. The cards always run for him. I don't know how he does it."

How do you suppose Cal does it?

7. "There's only one right way to play Poker," Biff says. "If you can't raise, drop out."

How do you propose to handle Biff?

8. "Nuts to the odds," Larry says. "I rely on common sense."

Do you think Larry's version of common sense makes him a winner?

9. "Poker is fun, and I enjoy being with this crowd," Ned says, "but I wish we were playing Pinochle tonight. Pinochle is a *real* test of skill."

"Ned is a killer at Pinochle," your host says.

Do you think it likely Ned is a killer at Poker, too?

10. Finally, the game is about to get under way, and the dealer announces, "Down the River."

Oscar fires a series of questions: "You mean Seven-Card Stud?" and, "One winner or high-low?" and "What's the ante?" and "Anything wild?" and "How much can a man bet on an open pair?" and so on. You know that Oscar, a group regular, should be familiar with its practices. Do you know why he is asking all these questions?

ANSWERS

1. It has been my experience that men who know how to acquire money and hang on to it usually extend that aptitude to Poker. Expect Josh to be competent and on the cautious side.

2. Chuck is a blowhard. Nobody repeatedly beats the percentages in the Nevada joints. Chuck will try to bull the game.

3. Mike is prudent and he sounds intelligent, unlike those who mouth the platitude "Always play for more than you can afford." Look for Mike to play strong, sound Poker.

4. Walter Johnson was a right-hander, not a southpaw. Marty never saw him pitch. Rely on Marty for misinforma-

tion on any subject which comes up, and for Poker strategy which is contrary to established principles.

5. Going to a baseball game is a simple matter, but not for Doc, who tries to make everything he tackles a Hollywood epic. He will fuddle and fuss and fume over every hand, confusing himself in the process.

Incidentally, Doc is odds-on, at 15 to 1, to be late Friday night, and not necessarily with a valid reason. If you go to the game with him, you will miss the first two innings.

6. Cal does it by playing the probabilities. A tough man.

7. Let Biff put that theory to the test, and trap him at every opportunity. He should be a pushover for you.

8. If Larry had more sense, common or uncommon, he would learn the basic odds of Poker. He has handicapped himself by evading that knowledge. Watch him squander his chips, and get your share of them.

9. Pinochle is, indeed, a game of skill which merits respect, but Ned's Poker technique undoubtedly does not. If he understood Poker, he would not, by implication, low-rate the unique skills it demands.

10. Oscar may be nervous — or he may be asking those questions to distract the opposition: a tactic. Don't listen to him. Just keep an eye on him to determine whether he is tense or tricky.

17

The Essential Rules

Being exceedingly pliable, Poker permits many variations, but the basic procedure is practically the same in all
of them and the essential rules are simple. If you do not
already know the rules, you can learn them in a few minutes. Thereafter, you can easily adapt them to whichever
variation is being played.

Poker requires no set number of players. In a pinch two
are enough. More players produce more action. Seven
usually make an ideal game. Most of the popular variations
can comfortably accommodate eight; some variations can
accommodate more.

This is the idea behind every variation: you hope to
accumulate a five-card hand which will outrank those held
by your opponents. The ranking of the hands is explained

in the next chapter, "The Structure of Poker."

While the purpose of Poker is to provide pleasure, the object is to win money. In each deal an amount of money, called the pot, is at stake. Usual practice is to start building the pot with an ante: each player puts up a designated amount, or each dealer in turn antes for the entire group.

The dealer shuffles the deck; the player immediately to his right cuts it. Then the dealer distributes the cards clockwise, one at a time to each player. The number of cards the dealer distributes at any stage depends on the variation. In any case, there are intervals or rounds of betting.

The science and art are in the betting. Bear in mind that Poker is a series of speculations — a series of financial operations, not card operations. "Playing the hand" is merely an idiom here; all you do with your cards is subject them to your own careful appraisal; then you *play your money* accordingly, as a threat or cudgel or snare or shield. You may, at any betting turn, drop out of the action so as to conserve your money for the next deal. There are three kinds of bets:

1. Opening bet — the first in a round.
2. Call — an equalizing bet; it must match the last previous bet by an opponent.
3. Raise — an aggressive bet greater than the last previous bet.

Almost always, a limit is clamped down on the amount which may be bet at one time. Be sure you understand the limit when you sit down to play. "Bet the raise," "pot limit," and "table stakes" are examples of dangerous limits (see "Glossary" at end of book).

At the conclusion of each deal, there is a final betting round. At the conclusion of the betting, if two or more players have stayed, that is, remained in the action, they show their hands; this is called the showdown. The holder of the highest ranking hand wins the pot. In high-low variations, the holder of the highest ranking hand divides the pot with the holder of the lowest ranking hand.

You can win a pot another way: when all your opponents drop out, conceding it to you. Sometimes you can achieve this with a bluff, with bold, risky betting which so intimidates the holders of higher ranking hands that they drop out.

Unless the last bet by the winner of a pot has been called, he is not required to reveal his hand. The principle: you must pay to see.

Poker has two fundamental forms, from which all the variations stem: in *Closed* Poker all the cards are dealt face down; in *Stud* Poker some cards are dealt face down, some open. Only the holder of a hand may look at the faces of the closed cards in it, prior to the showdown. A player who drops out prior to the showdown is not required to show his closed cards, except in one case which will be explained later.

The classical form of Closed Poker is Draw and the most enduring variation of Draw is Jackpots, which will serve here as our prototype. Jackpots is played under these rules:

Five cards, constituting the "original hand," are dealt to each player, and the betting begins. To open the betting, a player must hold "Jacks or better," that is, a hand which contains one pair of J's or a higher ranking combination. The holder of such a hand is not compelled to open; he may check, that is, decline to bet, while retaining the privilege of staying if an opponent should open.

Although there is no official rule against checking and then raising after an opponent has opened, most groups frown on the tactic (for reasons which elude me). On joining a new group, always inquire about check-and-raise betting; even though you may not intend to do it, you should be on guard against opponents who will.

All the action is clockwise: the player immediately to the dealer's left must act first and is said to be "under the gun." If the player under the gun does not open, the next player must act, and so on. If every player checks, the deal is passed out; then there is usually an additional ante, and the same variation is dealt again.

When the betting has been opened, each following player must in turn raise or call or drop out. If a following player raises, the opener may reraise. If, after a raise, the opener drops out, he may be required to show his opening combination: the exception to the rule about concealing closed cards.

The betting continues until equalized.

Now comes the "Draw." In turn, each stayer may try to improve his original hand by discarding from it and getting, from the undealt portion of the deck, replacements equal in number to his discards. A player may stand pat, may play the original hand as is, without drawing.

With less than six players at the table, a stayer may draw as many as five cards. With six or more at the table, the draw is usually limited to three cards.

If the opener discards from his opening combination, he must put those cards face down in the pot so that they may be inspected, if necessary, after the showdown.

The card at the bottom of the deck is never dealt. If the draw exhausts the deck, the discards and bottom card are shuffled and cut; then the draw continues from those cards.

After the draw comes the final betting round, under the same rules as the betting before the draw, except that the opener is under the gun. If the opener has been driven out

by a raise, the next player still in the action must bet or check. Most groups increase the limit for this betting round.

The deal ends with the showdown — and the closing ceremony in which the winner hauls in the pot.

Now that you know the procedure in Jackpots, see how easy it is to adapt yourself to other variations of Draw. Suppose, in a dealer's choice game, a dealer announces "Draw, anything opens." The announcement is self-explanatory: in turn, any player may open with any hand; otherwise there is no change in the rules.

Suppose a dealer announces "Blind Tiger." You request an explanation. He tells you, "The player after the dealer opens blind, and the next player straddles." This means that the first two players open and raise, respectively, before they get their cards. After the original hand has been dealt, the third player is under the gun in an automatically raised pot. Otherwise, there is no change in the rules.

Similarly, a brief explanation should enable you to proceed properly in any other variation of Draw.

Five-Card Stud is the original and traditional variation of the part-open form of Poker and will serve as our prototype. Some groups play Stud with an ante; some omit the ante.

In Five-Card Stud, the dealer starts by giving each player two cards, one face down and one open. The down card is called the "hole card," is said to be "in the hole."

After the first two cards have been dealt, the first betting round takes place. The holder of the highest open card may open the betting or check. If there is a tie, the high card holder nearest the dealer's left must act first. Otherwise the betting rules are the same as at Jackpots.

In subsequent betting rounds at Stud, the holder of the highest ranking open *combination* is under the gun. Example: the holder of a low pair must act before the holder of A K.

The remaining cards in Five-Card Stud are dealt open. Available to each stayer are:

A third card, followed by a betting round; a fourth card, followed by a betting round; a fifth card, followed by the final betting round and the showdown.

Usual practice at Stud is to raise the limit as soon as an open pair appears, or after the last card has been dealt.

In many variations of Stud, each player gets *two* cards in the hole and one open before the first betting round. In many variations, the last card is also dealt in the hole. A draw, usually limited to one card, may be incorporated. Such changes present new strategic and tactical problems, but the essential rules remain the same.

In variations which make more than five cards available to you, you play only the best combination of *five*.

I hope you will turn up the winning combination often in the showdown and I assure you it is not a matter of chance over the long haul.

18

The Structure of Poker

In descending order, the cards rank as follows: Ace, King, Queen, Jack, 10, 9, 8, 7, 6, 5, 4, 3, 2 — an arbitrary, and necessary, arrangement. When a deal starts, your chances of catching an A or a 2 are equal.

The classes of hands are another matter — the scarcer a class, the higher its rank. In descending order, the standard classes are:

Five of a kind:° Five cards of the same rank, possible only with the Joker or wild cards.

Straight flush: Five consecutive cards in one suit. The royal flushes, A K Q J 10, are the highest straight flushes.

Four of a kind: Four cards of the same rank.

Full house: Triplets and a pair. When full houses compete, the triplets determine the outcome. Example: 3 3 3

°See "Glossary", if necessary, for alphabetical listing of these and other terms.

4 4 wins over 2 2 2 A A.

Flush: Five cards, not consecutive, in the same suit.

Straight: Five consecutive cards, not in the same suit. An A may be used at the bottom of a 5-high straight: 5 4 3 2 A.

Triplets (three of a kind): Three cards of the same rank.

Two pairs: When hands containing two pairs compete, the higher top pair wins. If the top pairs are equal, the higher of the bottom pairs win. If both pairs are equal, the higher fifth card wins.

One pair: If competing pairs are equal, the highest side card wins.

Runt: No pair, below one pair. When runts compete, the highest card wins. Go down the line to break ties.

The following table shows how the ranking of the classes of hands carries out the law of supply and demand:

2,598,960 Hands Possible from 52-Card Deck

Hand		Number Possible	Frequency in Number of Hands	Odds against
Straight flush		40	1 in 64,974	64,973 to 1
Four of a kind		624	1 in 4,165	4,164 to 1
Full house		3,744	1 in 694	693 to 1
Flush		5,108	1 in 509	508 to 1
Straight		10,200	1 in 255	254 to 1
Triplets		54,912	1 in 47	46 to 1
Two pairs:	A's-up	19,008		
	K's-up	17,424		
	Q's-up	15,840		
	J's-up	14,256		
	10's-up	12,672		
	9's-up	11,088		
	8's-up	9,504		
	7's-up	7,920		
	6's-up	6,336		
	5's-up	4,752		
	4's-up	3,168		
	3's-up	1,584		
	Total two pairs	123,552	1 in 21	20 to 1
One pair (84,480 of each)		1,098,240	1 in 2.37	4 to 3

Runt:

A only high	A high or low			
A-high	A- or K-high	502,860		
K-high	Q-high	335,580		
Q-high	J-high	213,180		
J-high	10-high	127,500		
10-high	9-high	70,360		
9-high	8-high	34,680		
8-high	7-high	14,280		
7-high	6-high	4,080		
	Total runts	1,302,540	1 in 1.99	Even

Within the classes of hands, we find some important paradoxes.

The frequency is the same for a royal flush and a lower straight flush, the same for four A's and four 2's. Frequencies are the same, also, among the full houses, straights, triplets, and one pairs. Rank within each of these classes is consistent with the original ranking of the cards.

Among the flushes, we meet the first paradox: the higher the flush, the *greater* its frequency. This is not often a factor, the appearance of two or more flushes in the same deal is unusual.

Among the two pairs, we met a similar paradox, and here it materially influences tactics, because different two pairs often compete in the same deal. The higher the two pairs, the more frequency they are dealt. The inexperienced player may sometimes say to himself, "There are twelve subclasses among the two pairs, with 7's-up near the middle. Therefore, when I hold 8's-up, I figure to beat an opponent's two pairs." Such reasoning can lead to the use of a barrel as apparel. The two pairs, J's-up and higher, outnumber the two pairs, 10's-up and lower; yes, the top four subclasses outnumber the lower eight subclasses.

Among the runts, we meet the same sort of paradox: the higher the runt, the more frequently it is dealt. K-high and Q-high runts are common; 8-high and lower runts are scarce. This is the solid fact behind High-Low Poker.

The frequency of triplets or better in five cards is 1 in 35. The frequency of 8-high or lower in five cards is 1 in 49.

To jazz up the game, some groups use a stripped deck; they remove the 4's, 3's, and 2's. In addition to producing more "big hands," a deck so stripped introduces its own paradox, as you can see from this table:

658,008 Hands Possible from 40-Card Deck, Nothing Wild

Hand	Number possible	Frequency in number of hands	Odds against
Straight flush	28	1 in 235,000	234,999 to 1
Four of a kind	360	1 in 1,828	1,827 to 1
Full house	2,160	1 in 305	304 to 1
Flush	980	1 in 671	670 to 1
Straight	7,140	1 in 92	91 to 1
Triplets	23,040	1 in 29	28 to 1
Two pairs	51,480	1 in 13	12 to 1
One pair	322,560	1 in 1.7	Odds-on 10 to 7
Runt	249,900	1 in 2.6	3 to 2

The full houses outnumber the flushes, and some groups adjust the rankings accordingly, but most groups stick with tradition. Note also that the one pairs outnumber the runts.

Adding the wild Joker to the deck alters the structure of the game, as the following table shows:

2,869,685 Hands Possible from 53-Card Deck, Joker Wild

Hand	Number possible	Frequency in number of hands	Odds against
Five of a kind	13	1 in 220,745	220,744 to 1
Straight flush	204	1 in 14,067	14,066 to 1
Four of a kind	3,120	1 in 920	919 to 1
Full house	6,552	1 in 438	437 to 1
Flush	7,804	1 in 368	367 to 1
Straight	20,532	1 in 140	139 to 1
Triplets	137,280	1 in 21	20 to 1
Two pairs	123,552	1 in 23	22 to 1
One pair	1,268,088	1 in 2.26	1.26 to 1
Runt	1,302,540	1 in 2.2	Approx. even bet

The pat hands, including four of a kind, become more numerous but are still relatively scarce. When we reach the triplets and two pairs, we find a paradox: the triplets are more numerous than the two pairs but, because of tradition, the triplets continue to rank higher. Note that there can be no two pairs with the Joker.

Some groups use the Joker as the "Bug," rambunctious but not completely wild. It makes possible 2,869,865 hands. The Bug may be used only as an A, or as any card which fills a flush or a straight. For example, A A Bug 2 2 is a full house; Spade K J 8 5 Bug is a flush; 9 8 7 6, in different suits, Bug is a straight; A Bug J J 2 is two pairs, A's-up.

2,869,685 Hands Possible from 53-Card Deck with The Bug

Hand	Number possible	Frequency in number of hands	Odds against
Five aces	1	1 in 2,869,685	2,869,684 to 1
Straight flush	204	1 in 14,067	14,066 to 1
Four of a kind	828	1 in 3,466	3,465 to 1
Full house	4,368	1 in 657	656 to 1
Flush	7,804	1 in 368	367 to 1
Straight	20,532	1 in 140	139 to 1
Triplets	63,480	1 in 45	44 to 1
Two pairs	138,600	1 in 21	20 to 1
One pair	1,154,560	1 in 2.5	3 to 2
Runt	1,479,308	1 in 1.9	Approx. even bet

In most hands, the Bug is dead weight. In some situations, it is a useful defensive card: the holder can be sure it is not helping an opponent. The presence of the Bug produces the same proportion of straight flushes, flushes, and straights as does the wild Joker.

Especially notable is the way the Bug, in a hand with straight possibilities, shortens the odds in the draw. For example, 9 8 7 and the Bug will become a straight if it catches a J, 10, 6, or 5; it is a sixteen-chance hand. The odds against improvement are only 2 to 1.

Note that the odds against improving K Q J, or 4 3 2, to a straight are 3 to 1.

Similarly, the odds against improving a broken sequence of three cards and the Bug — 9 8 6 Bug, for example — are 3 to 1.

Many Draw and Stud variations are played with the Deuces wild: the weak become strong. The resulting structure is shown in the following table:

2,598,960 Hands Possible from 52-Card Deck, Deuces Wild

Hand	Number possible	Frequency in number of deals	Odds against
Five of a kind	672	1 in 3,868	3,867 to 1
Straight flush	4,556	1 in 570	569 to 1
Four of a kind	30,816	1 in 84	83 to 1
Full house	12,672	1 in 205	204 to 1
Flush	13,204	1 in 197	196 to 1
Straight	66,236	1 in 39	38 to 1
Triplets	355,056	1 in 7	6 to 1
Two pairs	95,040	1 in 27	26 to 1
One pair	1,222,048	1 in 2.13	Approx. even bet
Runt	798,660	1 in 3.25	2.35 to 1

The four of a kinds outnumber the full houses plus the flushes, and the triplets outnumber the two pairs. There is an appreciable reduction in the number of runts, because every runt which includes a 2 has become at least one pair.

Do not apply this table to variations in which the low hand wins. The wild Deuces make possible the conversion of many higher ranking hands to low runts. For example, A 2 2 2 2 is five A's in the table. At low-hand-wins, or High-Low, it can be called the lowest of the lows: 5 4 3 2 1 or 6 4 3 2 1.

Although Potzer has never concerned himself with the structure of the four-wild-card game, it is among his favorites. "How about something with the Deuces wild!" he says, as Mouse riffles.

"No, the Deuces are my jinx." Mouse gets the deck cut. "Every time I hypo the Deuces, I catch a pair of 3's."

"No problem," Guffy says. "Make the 3's wild; then you'll catch Deuces."

Mouse laughs sardonically. "That's the story of my life." He goes into a reverie, comes out of it with a hunch. "Down the River, with the Jacks wild."

"The one-eyed Jacks?" Showbuck asks.

"The one-eyed Jacks along with their flat-faced brothers," Mouse says. "All of them."

"Attaboy!" Potzer says.

"Jacks, tacks, wax, hacks." Wad crushes out a cigaret butt. "The percentages stay the same."

"How can they stay the same?" Pundit argues. "We're culling out four high cards and leaving in four low ones."

Wad shrugs. "You figure it your way, and I'll figure it my way."

Guffy breaks into song. "Ooooh, you'll take the high road, and . . ."

"Shove the opera." Potzer, agreeing with Pundit, asks confirmation from Brill. "What's the scoop on that, professor?"

Brill is diplomatic. "Pundit's reasoning is logical, as far as it goes," he says. "But carry it one step farther and you'll see Wad is right. With the Jacks wild, just move the 10's up one rank. Do the same with all the lower cards."

Potzer accepts the dictum without understanding it.

Pundit stares incredulously at Brill.

Wad says, "You could have skipped the lecture for all

it accomplished."

"Play cards," Showbuck barks. He has a Jack in the hole.

It is after midnight, and the game breaks up with Pundit wondering aloud what would happen if the A's were made wild.

"The Kings would become the highest natural cards," Brill patiently explains.

Now Pundit gets it!

Potzer has not been listening. "The game's at my home next week," he says. "See you there." He looks at you, including you in the invitation.

Tomorrow morning, Doris Wad will call your wife ,and will ask her to bring you to the party a week from Saturday night. If you are unattached, she will call you and suggest that you bring a Poker-playing girl friend.

Doris will provide a fine meal. She is a generous and gracious hostess. And she has a lulu of a variation cooked up for . . .

19

The Bisexual Poker Party

Doris feigns sleep as Wad gets into bed and tries to draw her close. Her sudden awakening is a performance which deserves an Oscar. "Huh! What time is it?"

"What's the difference, honey? Did you enjoy your game with the girls?"

"Sort of." She lies down again, heavily, on her side, with her back to him. "How'd you do?"

"Not too bad. Brill was the big winner."

"He's always lucky." She sighs. "I'm afraid I won't be able to fall asleep again."

"I'm sorry. Don't you like for me to hold you?"

"Uhuh, but I need my sleep."

Wad gives up. "Okay. G'night."

Doris scratches the back of her neck. "As long as I'm

awake, I may as well tell you what's cooking. I've asked the whole crowd here a week from Saddy."

"All fourteen?" At any hour, Wad's addition is rapid and accurate.

"Sixteen." Doris pulls away. "I'm asking that new player and his wife along with the rest."

"It'll cost a couple hundred bucks to feed that mob."

"We owe a lot of dinners." She lets her body tentatively touch his. "This way, we'll square all our obligations at one time."

Wad puts an arm about her. "I guess you're right." He appreciates her practicality, too.

"After we eat, we'll all play Poker, the husbands together with the wives." She takes his hand, brushes his fingers against her lips.

"Swell," he says.

"I knew you'd go for it, darling." She snuggles against him.

"Guess what that skinny, crummy Doris is planning." Like a savage sticking a pin in a voodoo doll, Terry stabs the ashtray with a cigaret butt. "A big dinner party, with Poker after the dinner."

"What'll the women do?" Showbuck asks.

"Play Poker *with* the men."

Showbuck makes a derisive noise in his throat. "Wiggle out of it. Tell her we've got another date."

"Not on your life. It was *my* idea in the first place. I was leading up to it when, all of a sudden, she spilled it like it was her own. I'm not gonna let anybody, least of all her, gyp me out of an evening of fun with my friends. If for no other reason, we'll go just out of spite."

Polly is waiting up for Pundit, and she has a glass of warm milk ready for him. As he drinks and the ache in his gut diminishes, she tells him about Doris's forthcoming party.

"The female of the species is more deadly than the male," Pundit says. He is thinking the men will find a way to foil the women and to have their usual stag game while the women break into Bridge foursomes.

Polly reads his mind. "We'll be a lot deadlier than that if you or any of those other baboons tries any nonsense."

"What's more nonsensical than a mixed Poker game?"

"The men herding off by themselves and refusing to let their wives share their fun. I should think you'd be glad to have the opportunity of teaching me the game."

"What do you want to know about it?"

"Well, for one thing, what's higher, a flush or a straight?"

"A flush."

"Why?"

"That's the rule."

Polly shrugs. "Then I'll have to try for flushes."

Pundit starts taking off his shoes. His gut is aching again.

"You should have heard the boys bleat last night," Guffy gloats at breakfast. "I really steamed them."

Mabel knows he had a moderate win. If he had lost, he would not be so cheerful; if he had won heavily, he would be gloating about that.

"I hope you didn't get Wad sore," she says.

"Why not? What's special about Wad?"

"Nothing, except that Doris has invited us to a shindig at their home. The whole crowd is going. The husbands and wives will play Poker together."

"Good one!" Guffy laughs loudly. "Will you please give

me that punch line again, sweetie?"

Although Mabel has expected some such response, she is a little hurt, and it shows in her eyes. "Don't you want to go?" It shows in her tone, too.

There is no meanness in Guffy. "Of course I want to go." He hugs her. "As a matter of fact, it oughta be fun — a 44-D bra full of fun."

When Caroline breaks the news to Mouse, he is in no position to protest or attempt witticisms. She can play any card game better than he, and they both know it. She is considerate enough to say, "You'll have to give me some Poker pointers."

"Oh, you understand the game."

"Yes, but I'm out of practice, dear. One of these evenings, we can deal out a few experimental hands, and you can help me brush up."

He beams. "Any time you say."

To Potzer, Poker is Poker; stag, bisexual — one kind is as good as another. "It'll be a nice way to spend a Saturday night," he says, "but do you think you can take care of yourself with that gang?"

"I'm sure they'll make the stakes low," Sue says, "so we can't get hurt much." Then, hopefully: "And, who knows, if we're lucky, we'll come out ahead."

They are two of a kind: their approach to card games is the same.

As Brill winces at the news, Gloria gives him a leathery pat on the cheek and says, "Neither do I detect any sense in it. I just *loathe* cards. How*ever*, I consider it politic *not* to rub Doris the wrong way. The Women's Civic Improvement Association is *hoping* to obtain a generous contribution from Wad."

"The Women's Association is drawing to an inside straight."

"You'll just have to *explain* to me about the advantages of inside straights and such things. Meanwhile, I am afraid we shall *have* to go."

"Okay."

"Anyhow, Doris always *does* serve a delectable meal."

Punctiliously, Gloria and Brill reach Wad's house at the appointed time. They see no cars parked there. Gloria, who is behind the wheel, steps on the gas. "I do not want to appear too eager." They kill fifteen minutes on the highways.

Caroline and Mouse are the first couple to enter.

Close behind them are Sue and Potzer.

A butler begins serving ornate canapes.

Mabel and Guffy enter a distant third.

Gloria and Brill are fourth.

Immediately after them come Polly and Pundit.

Terry and Showbuck finish a late and beaming last. Terry apologizes triumphantly.

Guffy has a new anecdote, a mild one about an amorous spinster from Biloxi.

"I wish I could remember stories," Mabel says.

Caroline remembers one about a rustic couple on their honeymoon in the hayloft, and hints the point across.

"Let's stop calling things by their nicknames," Terry says. She tells about the city boy who invited his country cousin to a burlesque show, and is prodigal with four-letter words. The women shriek, except Gloria who tries to achieve a Mona Lisa smile.

"That Terry is a card," Pundit says.

Showbuck is proud. He taps Terry on the shoulder. "Give 'em the one about the bearded lady . . . you know."

Terry gives it to them, with gestures. This time even Gloria joins in the laughter.

Polly effects the transition to the alimentary canal. Her story is a boffola.

The liquor flows and the stories get riper. Showbuck, with a reeker, tops them all.

"Party's getting rough," Sue says.

"Dinner is served," Doris says. It is served later than she had intended.

The dinner, featuring terrapin soup, venison, and wild duck, is relished and praised. Terry is notably lavish with her praise — and smug. She has just conceived a wonderful, wonderful idea: to serve pheasant under glass when she gives her party, and it is a secret she will keep well, even from Showbuck.

They dawdle over the dessert, three kinds. They dawdle over the coffee. They dawdle over the liqueurs. Potzer, eager to play Poker, says, "We're losing money. Deal, somebody."

Showbuck seconds the motion with a merry belch.

"Downstairs to the playroom, everybody," Doris says. "Hurry!"

Only Caroline and Potzer hurry. Wad remains at the dinner table to complete a dissertation on taxation: he is opposed to all forms of it. Gloria gives him rapt attention, preparatory to broaching the contribution on Monday. Polly explains the Blackwood Bridge convention to Sue. Mabel, who should not have taken that last liqueur, must lie down a while. Pundit says the tobacco smoke is murdering him; he goes out to the porch, where Polly follows with a show of tenderness. There are other delays and, all in all, the dinner-to-Poker interlude takes a half-hour.

In the playroom, two Poker tables have been set up, complete with decks of cards, chips, packages of cigarets, books of matches, bowls of fruit, and name cards. Potzer makes a last, brave effort to separate the sexes: he slyly starts shifting name cards . . .

Thwack! Doris brings the flat side of a fruit knife down on his knuckles. Potzer rubs the knuckles, contrives a smile, and retreats. Doris makes sure all the name cards are where she originally placed them. At one table, she has grouped your wife, Wad, Gloria, Mouse, Terry, Guffy, Polly, and Potzer. At the other table, she has grouped you, Sue, Pundit, Caroline, Brill, Mabel, Showbuck, and herself.

Before the games get under way, the men achieve a victory: the bowls of fruit are removed from the tables to the bar.

"How much are we playing for?" Sue asks cautiously.

Showbuck, who makes a practice of talking out of turn, answers, "The usual stakes, I suppose."

"Don't be such a big shot," Polly says.

Terry, loyal to her husband, shoots a scornful look at Polly.

While Showbuck fumbles in his mind for a retort which will be fitting and yet make allowance for Polly's sex, Brill says, "Let's play for the usual stakes, but settle for only fifty percent. That way, we'll get all the excitement, but nobody will be hurt financially."

The women accept the principle, without the fifty percent proviso. They decide to settle for twenty percent.

The games start tamely with the traditional variations of Draw and Stud. No big hands are dealt, and the women soon remedy that deficiency.

"Treys and Deuces wild," Terry says when it is her turn

to deal. "Seven-Card Stud, and if enough people drop out, I'll make it eight cards."

A few deals later, Polly has an improvement: "Treys and Deuces wild, but an open 7 kills you."

Wad is incredulous. "Will you give me that again, please?"

"An open 7 in your hand means you've got to fold."

"Why?"

"Because it's my deal."

She deals it. Terry, catching five A's in the first five cards, bets heavily. With everybody staying, a big pot is built up. Terry's sixth card is a 7.

Polly who has four K's is ecstatic. "You're killed."

"In a pig's eye!" Terry flicks aside the 7. "I had my five A's before you fixed me with that stupid card. You can't take them away from me."

"I can't, honeychile," Polly coos, "but the rules can."

Terry mumbles something about stupid rules and angrily folds her hand. Polly serenely continues the deal, betting her four K's aggressively. She fails to improve, but Potzer catches five 4's and hauls in the pot.

"Not such a smart variation after all," Polly says.

At the other table, Brill roguishly deals "Spit in the Ocean," a form of Draw in which all four cards of a rank are wild, producing a plethora of big hands. That is Doris's cue to deal a related variation which she, herself, has invented and saved for this occasion: "Spit in Outer Space," with all thirteen cards of one suit wild. It soon catches on at both tables, and for the rest of the evening everybody deals it. The women deal it because they love it; the men deal it because the women become petulant whenever a change is suggested.

Through it all, Potzer enjoys a phenomenal run. As usual,

he stays in every deal. As unusual, he catches one winning hand after another. The women rub his hair for luck. They consult him about dubious hands. They applaud his bravery when he succeeds with an outrageous bluff.

The men, too, are glad to see Potzer accumulate so many chips; they remain aware of the fact that the settlement will be on the basis of twenty percent. It will detract little from Potzer's pleasure. Tonight he is the champion, and the ultimate conversion of many chips into few bills cannot alter that.

Another hand is dealt and Potzer again catches five A's.

"This Outer Space is terrific," he squeaks. "We'll have to give it a try at our stag game."

None of the men answers him. At the proper moment, they will restore him to his accustomed place on our planet.

At 1:05 A.M., Polly, who has lost her fifth stack of chips and is unwilling to lose more, yawns and drawls, "I'm s-o-o-o-o tired."

Pundit decides he, too, is tired and cashes in his chips.

Gloria points out to Brill that they have a big Sunday ahead of them.

"I've enjoyed the game," Brill lies. He gives all his chips to Gloria.

The game breaks up. Doris gets praise for bringing the husbands and wives together at play, as in the good old days.

"We'll do it again one week from tonight at my house," Terry says.

Everybody accepts — except perhaps you and your wife. So there will be another evening of bisexual Poker, and a third, but there will be no fourth, because disintegration has already set in.

Showbuck will not forget the sneering way Polly called

him a big shot, and Terry will be sure Polly bilked her out
of a big pot. Acrimony between these couples is inevitable.

Gloria will get only a token contribution from Wad, and
will stop catering to Doris. She and Brill may appear at
Terry's party, but they will evade the one after that.

Guffy, who kept his needle in a sheath tonight, will un-
sheath it next week. He will jab it into the women as well
as the men. The women will be resentful.

Caroline prefers Bridge to Poker. So does Mabel. Over
Terry's protests, they will persuade Doris and Polly to play
at least one rubber with them.

Sue will lose more money at Poker than she does at
Bridge and will decide to leave the Poker to Potzer.

Whoever gives the third party will, after tallying the
cost, decide it is futile to try to keep up with the Wads
and the Showbucks.

The bisexual Poker cannot last in this group or in any
other.

And why should it last? Every feminine invasion must
eventually fail. Poker is a stag game.

Glossary

AGE — Also *edge;* the player immediately to the dealer's left.

ALTERNATE STRAIGHT — Also *Dutch straight, skip straight, skipper;* a sequence by twos. Example: J 9 7 5 3. Not a standard hand.

ANTE — Also *edge.* The amount put into the pot by each player, or by the dealer for the entire group, before the deal starts. Verb: to put in said amount.

AROUND-THE-CORNER STRAIGHT — A sequence of five cards with an A between the extremes. Example: 3 2 A K Q. Also *rounder, round-the-corner straight.* Not a standard hand.

BACK IN — To bet after having checked.

BACK-TO-BACK — A wired pair: a pair consisting of the first two cards in the hand.

BASEBALL — An intricate form of Stud, involving 9's, 4's, and 3's. See page 137.

BEAT THE BOARD — Also *beat the table;* to hold a better hand than any showing elsewhere.

BET — To put chips or cash into the pot after the deal has begun.

BET BLIND — To bet before looking at one's cards.

BET INTO — To bet before a player whose open cards or previous action indicate he may hold a better hand.

BET THE LIMIT — To bet the maximum amount permitted.

BET THE RAISE — A limit which permits a player to raise by the maximum amount previously bet at one time. Example: Amos bets two chips; Bob may bet four; if Bob does so, Chick may bet eight.

BIG CAT — Also *Big Tiger;* a hand consisting of five cards from the K down to the 8, unpaired. Not a standard hand.

BIG DOG — A hand consisting of five cards from the A down to the 9, unpaired. Not a standard hand.

BIG SQUEEZE — Also *Six-Card Option;* Six-Card High-Low Stud with one draw. See page 101.

BIG TIGER — See *Big Cat.*

BLAZE — A hand containing two pairs and consisting of five picture cards; ranked above A's-up in some groups. Not standard practice.

BLIND — The bet before the deal at Blind Tiger; the player who opens blind; any bet made without looking at one's cards.

BLIND TIGER — A form of Draw in which the age opens blind. Also *Open Blind,* or *Open Blind and Straddle.*

BLUFF — To bet aggressively on a hand one does not believe to be the best in the deal.

BOBTAIL — Also *bobtailed straight;* four consecutive cards open at both ends. Example: K Q J 10. Also *double-end straight* or *open-end straight* or *two-way straight.*

BUG — The Joker used only as an A, or to fill a flush or a straight.

BULLET — Also *bull;* an A.

BULL THE GAME — To bluff repeatedly. In some localities, to play aggressively throughout, regardless of one's hands. In high-stake games, to try to dominate by means of a bankroll big enough to call any bet.

BUMP — To bet an amount greater than that put up by the last preceding bettor in a round; also *kick it, raise, up it.*

BURN A CARD — To expose it, then insert it in the deck or put it at the bottom.

BURY A CARD — To insert it in the deck.

BUST — A worthless hand.

CALL — To put in the pot an amount equal to the last preceding bet.

CASE CARD — Also *caser;* a term borrowed from Faro; the last card of a rank or suit in the deal.

CATCH — To get a particular card or hand.

CHASE — To stay against a better hand.

CHECK — To pass an opportunity to open the betting; this reserves the right to back in if an opponent opens.

CHICAGO — A form of Stud in which the highest Spade in the hole wins half of the pot. Also named after other cities, in some localities.

CHIP — A disc used to represent money. Verb: to put chips in the pot.

CHIP DECLARATION — At High-Low, to use chips to indicate whether you are going for high or low or both.

CINCH HAND — Also *lock;* a hand which is sure to win the pot.

CLOSED HAND — A hand dealt with all the cards face down.

CLOSED GAME — A game to which no additional players will be admitted.

COLD HANDS — Complete hands dealt without intervening bets.

COUNTER — A chip; one who habitually counts one's chips or cash.

CUT — After the shuffle, to divide the deck into packets and change their order.

CUT THE GAME — In gaming establishments, to take an amount out of every pot.

DEAD HAND — A hand which, for any reason, may not be played.

DEAL — To distribute the cards to the players.

DEALER'S CHOICE — The right of the dealer, by agreement of the players, to name the variation which will be played when he deals.

DEAL OUT — To omit a player from the deal.

DECK — Also *pack;* all the cards used in the game.

DECLARE — At High-Low, to announce or indicate whether going for high or low or both.

DEUCE — Any 2.

DOUBLE-END STRAIGHT — See *bobtail.*

DOWN CARD — A card dealt face down.

DOWN THE RIVER — Seven-Card Stud. See page 73.

DRAW — Certain forms of the game; the cards delt to replace discards. Verb: to discard and take replacements from the dealer.

DRIVER'S SEAT — The situation of a player whose open cards, previous betting, or draw suggest he may hold the winning hand.

DROP — Also *drop out, fold, turn over;* to retire from a pot. Also, in some localities, the last card dealt to a player.

DUTCH STRAIGHT — See *alternate straight.*

EDGE — See *age, ante.*

FACE CARD — Also *picture card;* K Q or J.

FACED CARD — A card with its face down.

FATTEN — Also *sweeten;* to put more chips or cash in the pot.

FILL — To catch a card which improves the hand.

FIVE-CARD OPTION — Also *Little Squeeze;* Five-Card High-Low Stud with a draw.

FIVE OF A KIND — In wild-card variations, a hand consisting of five cards of the same rank.

FLASH — To expose a card.

FLIP — Also *Mexican Stud;* a five-card variation in which the optional hole card and all open cards of the same rank in a player's hand are wild.

FLUSH — A hand containing five cards, not consecutive, in the same suit.

FOLD — See *drop.*

FOLLOW THE QUEEN — A form of Stud in which the Q's, and cards of the same rank as the last card dealt open after a Q, are wild.

FOUR FLUSH — A hand containing four cards in the same suit.

FOUR OF A KIND — A hand containing four cards of the same rank.

FREE RIDE — Playing without being compelled to pay.

FREEZE-OUT — A game which a player must leave on losing a previously designated amount.

FULL HOUSE — Also *full hand;* triplets and a pair.

HAND — The cards dealt to a player.

HIGH-LOW — Any variation in which, as declared, the highest hand wins half of the pot and the lowest hand wins the outer half. An odd chip goes to the high winner.

HOLE — At Stud, the cards which are dealt face down, and remain so until the showdown; such a card is a hole card, or in the hole.

IMMORTAL — The best possible hand, high or low, in a variation.

INSIDE STRAIGHT — A broken sequence of four cards in a hand. Example: K Q 10 9.

JACKPOTS — The most popular form of Draw; a player must hold one pair of J's or better to open the betting. See page 23.

JACKSON — Also *Jacks and Back, Jacks and Reverse;* a form of Draw in which a deal starts out as Jackpots; if nobody opens, the deal becomes Lowball.

JOKER —A wild card added to the deck.

JUDGE DUFFY — Also any other judge; also *thirty days:* three 10's.

KEENO — Also *Klondike;* Six-Card Stud. See page 61.

KEEP HIM HONEST — To call a player suspected of bluffing.

KIBITZER — A spectator.

KICKER — A side card held with a pair or triplets when drawing.

KICK IT — See *bump.*

KILTER — Any of several nonstandard hands; see *Pelter.*

KITTY — Money accumulated by taking a stipulated amount from every pot.

KLONDIKE — Also *Keeno;* Six-Card Stud.

KNAVE — The Jack.

LIGHT — To play without immediately paying.

LIMIT — The maximum amount a player may bet.

LITTLE CAT — Also *Little Tiger;* a hand containing five cards from the 8 down to the 3, unpaired, Not a standard hand.

LITTLE DOG — A hand containing five cards from the 7 down to the 2, unpaired. Not a standard hand.

LITTLE SQUEEZE — See *Five-Card Option.*

LOCK — See *cinch hand.*

LOWBALL — A form of Draw in which the lowest hand wins the entire pot. See page 45.

LOW HOLE CARD WILD — A form of Stud in which the lowest hole card and all open cards of the same rank in a hand are wild. See page 131.

MATCHING CARD — A card of the same rank as another in a hand.

MATCH THE POT — To put up an amount equal to that already there.

MEXICAN STUD — See *Flip.*

MISDEAL — An improper deal.

MONKEY FLUSH — Three cards, not in sequence, in the same suit.

MOUTH BET — A bet made without putting up chips. It is binding.

NATURAL — A card which is not wild; a variation or hand without wild cards.

OFFICE HOURS — A straight from the 9 to the 5; two pairs, 9's and 5's.

ONE-END STRAIGHT — Also *one-way straight;* four cards in sequence, open at only one end: A K Q J, or 4 3 2 A.

ONE-EYED JACKS — The Spade and Heart J's; they are always drawn in profile.

ONE-EYED KING — The Diamond K; he is always drawn in profile.

OPEN — To open the betting; a card with its face up; a vacant seat; a game which will admit additional players.

OPEN BLIND — See *Blind Tiger.*

OPENERS — A holding with which a player is permitted to open the betting; usually one pair of J's or better at Jackpots.

ORIGINAL HAND — The cards dealt to a player before the draw.

PACK — The deck.

PAIR — Two cards of the same rank in a hand.

PASS — To drop when it is one's turn to bet; sometimes erroneously used as a synonym for *check.*

PASS-OUT — A form of the game in which checking is prohibited; a player must, in his turn, bet or drop.

PAT — A hand to which a player does not draw.

PELTER — Also called *Kilter;* a hand containing 9 5 2, with one card between the 9 and 5, and another card between the 5 and 2. Not a standard hand.

PICTURE CARD — Also *face card;* a K, Q, or J.

PINK — A Diamond or Heart flush.

PIP — A symbol on the face of a card, exclusive of corner indices, indicating the suit.

POT — The money at stake in a deal.

POT LIMIT — A limit which permits a player to bet an amount up to that already in the pot.

PROFILES — The Diamond K, Spade J, and Heart J.

PUT UP — To put money in a pot as required.

RAISE — See *bump.*

REDEAL — Another deal by the same dealer after one which was nullified.

RIFFLE — To shuffle the cards by dividing the deck into two packets, placing them end to end, and intermingling the cards at random with a movement of the fingers.

ROODLES — A special pot or series of pots at increased stakes.

ROUND-THE-CORNER STRAIGHT — See *around-the-corner straight.*

ROYAL FLUSH — A hand containing the A K Q J 10 in the same suit.

ROYALTIES — Premiums paid by all the players, as previously agreed, to the holder of a big hand, usually four of a kind or a straight flush without wild cards.

RUNT — A pairless hand below one pair.

SANDBAG — To check and then raise if an opponent opens the betting; in some localities, any method of luring more chips into the pot rather than by force by raising.

SHORT — Lacking a sufficient amount; also *shy*.

SHORT PAIR — A pair lower than J's.

SHOTGUN — Draw, with the dealing of the original hand interrupted after the third card to interpolate a round of betting.

SHOWING — Open cards.

SHOWDOWN — After the completion of a deal and the betting, showing the hands to determine the winner.

SHUFFLE — To mix the cards prior to cutting and dealing.

SHY — See *short*.

SIDE CARD — Any card in a hand apart from a class. Example: 8 8 8 4 3; the 8's are triplets; the 4 and 3 are side cards.

SIDE MONEY — At table stakes, an amount set apart from the main pot.

SIX-CARD OPTION — Also *Big Squeeze;* Six-Card High-Low Stud with a draw. See page 101.

SKEET — See *Pelter*.

SKIPPER — See *alternate straight*.

SKIP STRAIGHT — See *alternate straight*.

SNOW — To bluff or to fake.

SPIT IN THE OCEAN — Also *Spit in the River;* any of numerous variations in which cards turned up in the center of the table may be used simultaneously by all the players. See page 121.

SPIT IN THE RIVER — See *Spit in the Ocean*.

SPLIT OPENERS — To discard from a class with which it is permissable to open, usually from one pair at Jackpots.

SPLIT PAIR — Two cards of the same rank, one in the hole, one open.

STACK — A pile of chips.

STACK THE DECK — To arrange the cards in known places.

STAND-OFF — A tie.

STAND PAT — To decline an opportunity to draw.

STAY — To continue in a deal.

STEAL THE POT — To win it with a bluff, or to win it with an inferior hand by default as the opposition drops.

STRADDLE — A compulsory raise before the deal at Blind Tiger.

STRAIGHT — A hand containing five cards in sequence.

STRAIGHT DRAW — A form of Draw in which any player, in his turn, may open the betting with any hand.

STRIPPED DECK — A deck from which low cards have been removed, usually 4's, 3's, and 2's.

STUD — Any form of the game in which one or more cards are dealt in the hole to a player, and the rest of his cards are dealt open.

SUDDEN DEATH — Five-Card High-Low Stud. See page 108.

SWEETEN — See *fatten*.

TABLE STAKES — A limit which permits a player, in any betting turn, to put up all the chips he has on the table; this is called *tapping*. He may not, during a deal, buy more chips or remove any from the table. If an opponent wants to call but cannot match such a bet, he must put up all the chips he has on the table. Example: Andy taps for one hundred chips, and Bert calls for that amount. Tom, who has only sixty chips on the table, puts them up. Forty of Andy's chips and forty of Bert's are set aside: they constitute the *side money*. If Tom wins the pot, he cannot claim the side money. By prearrangement, the side money is divided between Andy and Bert, or the holder of the better hand takes it.

TAP — At table stakes, to bet the limit.

THIRTY DAYS — See *Judge Duffy*; three 10's.

THREE OF A KIND — Also *triplets*; three cards of the same rank in a hand.

TREY — Any 3.

TRIPLETS — See *three of a kind*.

TWO PAIRS — A hand containing two pairs of different rank.

UNDER THE GUN — A situation in which a player must act before the others.

UP — Designating the higher of two pairs. Example: A's-up.

UP CARD — Also *open card*. A card dealt or turned face up.

VERBAL BET — See *mouth bet*.

WASH — To shuffle.

WHIPSAW — To raise before and behind a stayer. Usually, it is honest: each of the raisers believes he will win, while the sandwiched stayer hangs on with a mediocre hand. It may indicate collusion betwen the raisers: a common method of cheating.

WILD CARD — Usually a card which may represent any card in the deck at the holder's option. Its powers may be limited, as in the case of the *Bug*.

WIRED — A back-to-back pair; or the cards in any other class dealt consecutively, beginning with the first card.

WOOLWORTH — Any variation in which the 10's and 5's are wild.

The AUTHOR

IRWIN STEIG, born in 1901, insists that he has actually lived more than the elapsed number of years, because he has never wasted much time sleeping. While still a schoolboy he made the acquaintance of Poker, was fascinated by its probability problems, became a lightning calculator of odds. But he laughs off any suggestion that he is a gambler, and as a practitioner of Poker has been demonstrating over the years that in all its forms it is a pure test of skill.

Director of public relations for a Connecticut chemical manufacturing company, he also finds time for writing which runs the gamut from satirical fiction to articles on technical subjects, usually with a humorous slant.

At the Poker table he can outlast anybody he has ever met. He revels in long sessions which often leave the opposition in a state of shock. When such a session ends, he is likely to seek out somebody with whom he can play fast chess, another game at which he excels.

WILLIAM STEIG, a younger brother of the author, is a preeminent humorous artist of our era. His drawings in *The New Yorker* and other magazines, pointing out the foibles of humanity, have made millions laugh. His books of symbolic drawings have probed the mind, the spirit, in a new genre.

The ILLUSTRATOR

To this book, as to Irwin's earlier and classical *Poker for Fun and Profit*, William has contributed a series of delightful illustrations.

"I tell Bill a few things about a Poker player he has never seen," Irwin says, "and in a few simple lines that character is on paper as he looks and acts. It's uncanny."

The brothers, who have the same outlook on life, disagree on one subject. William, a college all-America water polo player back at age 16, is still a powerful swimmer. Irwin, whose idea of aquatic sport is a hot shower, argues, "It took life aeons to emerge from the sea. Why go back?"